Effective Preaching As Paul Did It

By

Sam Binkley, Jr.

ISBN 1-58427-167-1

Table of Contents

Preface

He was falsely accused and brought before the Jewish council to answer the charges. The high priest asked him if the things were true. The answer he gave began with a reminder of the promise that the God of glory gave to their father Abraham. During the course of his speech he showed how the Jews as a whole did not obey the living oracles which Moses received at Mt. Sinai. He charged them with persecuting the prophets and slaying those who showed them before of the coming of the Just One, and failing to keep the law. They were angered at Stephen's message and stoned him to death. Among those present was a young man at whose feet the witnesses laid down their clothes. This man's name then was Saul, who also was consenting unto his death. Some time later he was converted to Christ and came to be known by the name of Paul. Many believe he became the most outstanding preacher of all time. Beginning in chapter thirteen of the Book of Acts and continuing through the rest of the Book we have detailed accounts of the preaching he did in much of the then known world. By reading what Luke wrote of his work we can learn a great deal that will help us be more effective preachers and teachers of the word of God. Paul also wrote letters to churches and individuals in which he tells us what he preached, how he preached, and why he preached as he did. No doubt he understood better than most why God chose the foolishness of preaching to save them that believe (1 Cor. 1:21).

Sam Binkley, Jr.

Dedication

To my lovely wife of more than sixty-seven years, **Rebecca Brown Binkley**, who sacrificed much to encourage me during the sixty plus years of preaching the gospel, I cheerfully dedicate this book. For the kind of person she is I offer this tribute:

In the Bible it says she's hard to find
A worthy woman that's good and kind
Mindful of others who are poor and in need,
Their hungry mouths she's ready to feed.

Her children are blessed, and her husband, too
She's known for her will to say and do.
Her affections are set on things above,
While imparting to all a spirit of love.

All who know her praise her good name,
Not for her fortunes and not for her fame.
But for the fear she has for the Lord,
And respect for the laws in his Holy Word.

I found her many years ago,
When jobs were few and salaries low.
I knew she was a special girl,
Worth more to me than all the world.

Lives are many she has blessed
By her kind deeds and unselfishness.
She goes beyond the second mile
To calm a fear and bring a smile.

She accepted me for better or worse,
Keeping her eyes on a steady course.
Earthly fame is not her goal,
She looks to heaven, the home of the soul.

Sam Binkley, Jr.
July 31, 1993

Introduction

In this modern age preachers generally are not respected and admired. Movies and TV programs usually portray them as hypocrites or fanatics. In real life, well-known preachers have done some exceptionally nutty things. Notwithstanding, young men should be encouraged to devote their lives to preaching the gospel.

Reading the manuscript of this book impressed me that the author says some things that are needed by old and young alike, particularly by those who aspire to preach and by those who are yet young in years. The seven chapters of the book, like the author's sermons, are filled with Scripture. Although an octogenarian with more than sixty years of experience in preaching, the author does not draw from his personal experiences as the basis for what he writes. He draws from the apostle Paul.

The book is an excellent review of much of Paul's life from the time of his conversion to the time that his departure was at hand. Paul's whole life as a disciple of Jesus was wrapped up in his preaching. If ever there was an effective preacher among Christ's followers, Paul was the man.

The reader of this book will be impressed that effective preaching begins with the right message. God told the prophet Jonah to preach *"the preaching that I bid thee"* (Jonah 3:2). Paul's message was that which was Christ's bidding. No matter how eloquent the preacher, how charming his personality, how entertaining and popular he may be, he is not effective according to God's standard unless he preaches what Paul preached.

Many of us who are older in years have genuine concern that a sizeable number of younger men are preaching very little Bible. They fill their sermonettes with interesting stories and illustrations, making people feel good about themselves, but their preaching does not have the distinctive ring of pure New Testament Christianity.

I am honored to introduce this book by my esteemed brother and friend, Sam Binkley, Jr. Preacher friend, read this book and ask yourself, *"How effective is my preaching?"*

Irvin Himmel

Chapter One

What Is Effective Preaching?

In some ways the responsibility of preaching Christ to a world so full of sin is like a father taking on the task of bringing up his children in the nurture and admonition of the Lord. In many cases both begin when one is ill prepared for the job before him. Skills and ability to effectively do the work can be developed by those who commit themselves to fulfill their God-given responsibility in any righteous endeavor. Everyone who commits himself to preaching the gospel of Christ should want to be as effective as he can be. To accomplish this purpose one must remember the charge Paul gave Timothy to *"preach the word."*

A casual look at the title of this book may cause some to conclude the author considers himself an effective preacher of the gospel. This is not the case, however, but rather a realization that we have a divine record of one who, in the eyes of the Lord, was very effective in preaching the gospel of our salvation. This book is not about the way I preach or have preached, but about the way Paul, an inspired apostle, preached. For preaching to be effective it must accomplish the purpose for which God gave it. This means it must convict the sinner of his guilt of sin, instruct him in what he must do to obtain forgiveness, and how to walk in newness of life, and then exhort him to do that. A careful study of both the subject matter of Paul's preaching, and the manner in which he proclaimed God's word will convince the honest student of the effectiveness of this great preacher. The measure of his effectiveness is not determined by men's standards. If that were the case he would have been a miserable failure for he was not the crowd pleaser many desired then, and who are the most popular preachers of today. Some even considered his speech contemptible.

Paul was a man of great ability intellectually, and combined this with unmistakable love and care for the souls of those he sought to teach, a rare commodity among men of any age. He made it a point to know what his audience needed and preached that in a way they could easily understand. He came in contact with a sorcerer who sought to turn one away from the faith and did not hesitate to use his apostolic authority to cause blindness to come upon him for a season. The one he sought to turn away *"saw what was done, believed, being astonished at the doctrine of the Lord"* (Acts 13:8-12). When he came to Athens he found the people wholly given to idolatry and preached to them the God they did not know (Acts 17:15ff). To Felix, a man given to fulfilling the desires of the flesh, he *"reasoned of righteousness, temperance, and the judgment to come"* (Acts 24:24-25). Agrippa was familiar with the prophets so Paul appealed to him on that basis, acknowledging the help he received from the Lord and saying only the things the prophets and Moses said should come (Acts 26:19-27).

Many who aspire to preach the unsearchable riches of Christ look to someone they have known, heard, or read after as an example they would like to imitate. Some hear an experienced preacher analyze an argument some false teacher has made on a certain passage of Scripture and are impressed with his ability to give a clear explanation of the truth on the matter, and desire to preach like that. Not everyone has that ability. Some will look to the ability of one to move an audience to respond to the call of the gospel, others to the ability of another to preach the truth plainly and illustrate it in such an effective way that it would be difficult to misunderstand it. This can be an excellent way to learn some valuable lessons about how to be an effective messenger of the Lord. There are those who have great ability to preach the gospel in such an effective manner, but I have never known anyone who was as effective as was Paul the great apostle. Role models can have a very positive impact on our lives if we recognize that they are just that, role models, and incorporate their good points, but still be ourselves rather than trying to be someone else. Surely all of us who enter into the work of preaching the gospel would like to be able to preach like Paul. We should want to give a clear understanding of the place and importance of the gospel in God's great scheme of redemption for sinful man. But we should never overlook the fact we have the perfect example in Jesus Christ, the Son of God.

Anyone who desires to preach the gospel of Jesus Christ should seek to learn all he can about what it means to be effective, and how he can be effective in winning souls to Christ. In the eyes of men what constitutes the work of an evangelist differs from one generation to another and from one culture to another. Consequently, ideas of his effectiveness may be measured by different standards. It should be obvious to the serious Bible student that effective preaching must include effective presentation of the truth resulting in changes in the lives of the hearers. God chose preaching as the means by which to save believers (1 Cor. 1:21). Elsewhere in the Scriptures we learn that it is the truth of the gospel presented in a clear and understandable way that will accomplish this. It is the gospel of Christ that is the power of God unto salvation to everyone who believes (Rom. 1:16). Preaching a perverted gospel will not accomplish this purpose, but will result in the cutting off of those who do so, whether men or angels. Paul, the apostle whose preaching we are considering in this book wrote, *"But though we, or an angel from heaven, preach any other gospel unto you than that which we have preached unto you, let him be accursed. As we said before, so say I now again. If any man preach any other gospel unto you than that ye have received, let him be accursed"* (Gal. 1:8-9). The manner in which the gospel is preached is also important as illustrated in the preaching Paul and Barnabas did in the synagogue in Iconium. They *"so spake, that a great multitude both of Jews and also of the Greeks believed"* (Acts 14:1).

Ultimately the effectiveness of a preacher's work will be known at the judgment of Jesus Christ. The apostle Paul likens the work of a preacher to one who builds on a foundation with gold, silver, precious stones, wood, hay, stubble. He then says that every man's work will be made manifest (become clear, made known for what it is) for it will be tried by fire. It will be a great occasion of rejoicing for the man whose work abides (1 Cor. 3:12-15). With some the work of a preacher is looked upon in much the same way as they view professional engineers, doctors, lawyers, teachers, etc. This results in some judging the effectiveness of preachers on the basis of their popularity with the members of the church. If they like him as a person, and he presents himself well in the pulpit, to them he is effective; if not, then he is not effective regardless of how much truth he preaches, and how much error he exposes. *What some are looking for in a preacher is his ability to operate a church smoothly rather than how much truth he knows and can communicate to the people, and backs up his teaching by a godly life.* The "social gospel" concept has a great influence on this kind of thinking. Growing out of this is also the practice of specialization such as ministers of music, education directors, youth ministers, and the like.

Good ministers of Jesus Christ put the brethren in mind of the fact that some depart from the faith, and in some ways this is done (1 Tim. 4:1-6). As servants of God they work for God and with his people. Paul told Timothy to do the work of an evangelist, which refers to one who bears good news (2 Tim. 4:5). His work, therefore, is to proclaim the good news of Christ our Savior both privately and publicly (Acts 20:20). His work among the children of God is designed to perfect them, bring them to a state of spiritual maturity, for the work of the ministry, that the body of Christ might be edified (Eph. 4:11-12). All children of God are laborers together with God, building upon the foundation of Jesus Christ, which was laid by the apostles (1 Cor. 3:9-11; Eph. 2:20). Having a desire to please God uppermost in his mind, the servant of God is careful to preach only the gospel that came by the revelation of Jesus Christ (Gal. 1:10-12).

A good way to measure the effectiveness of teachers of the word of God is to look at those whom they have taught. Effective teachers cause learning to take place in their students. Of course this does not mean all will fully accept the teaching and change their lives to conform to what was taught. Jesus, the Master Teacher, did not convince all who heard him that his doctrine was the only one that would save their souls. Those who have honest and good hearts are the ones whose lives will be changed by the truth when taught by an effective teacher. There are many examples that bear testimony to this fact. Some of these are found in the Bible, and no doubt we could name some among our personal acquaintances.

The effectiveness of a preacher of today is not determined by the number of large local churches he has worked with, the number of "gospel meetings" he preaches in each year, the number of debates he may have participated in, how many people he may have baptized, or the number of years he has been involved in the work; but rather whether or not he has fulfilled his ministry by preaching the word in season and out of season, reproving, rebuking, and exhorting with all longsuffering and doctrine (2 Tim. 4:1-5).

Another reason Paul was effective in his preaching was that he *"reasoned with them out of the scriptures"* (Acts 17:2). This was the occasion when Paul went to the city of Thessalonica and preached to the Jews as they met in the synagogue three Sabbath days. Using the Scriptures he explained and demonstrated to them that Jesus had to suffer and to rise from the dead, and that this Jesus was the Christ. While in prison in Rome Paul called for the chief of the Jews and told them that it was for the hope of Israel that he was bound with a chain. They said they had not heard anything against him, and that they wanted to know what he thought. At a set time *"he expounded and testified the kingdom of God, persuading them concerning Jesus, both out of the law of Moses, and out of the prophets, from morning till evening"* (Acts 28:23). He knew full well that Christ is the central theme of all acceptable preaching, and that the most effective way to convince the people that Jesus of Nazareth was the Christ was the Scriptures, both the law and the prophets. Who among those who preach the gospel today would presume to improve on the way this great preacher went about his work?

The Scriptures that explain and demonstrate that Jesus is the Christ are abundant. There is no other source that produces the kind of faith that leads to salvation than the Scriptures inspired of God. The Bible plainly says that faith comes by hearing and hearing by the word of God (Rom. 10:17). Jesus said the Scriptures testify of him. He said to the Jewish leaders, *"Search the scriptures, for in them ye think ye have eternal life, and they are they which testify of me"* (John 5:39). Paul wrote that he preached in the manner in which he did that the faith of those who heard him might not stand in the wisdom of men, but in the power of

God (1 Cor. 2:5). John wrote, *"And many other signs truly did Jesus in the presence of his disciples, which are not written in this book: But these are written, that ye might believe that Jesus is the Christ, the Son of God; and that believing ye might have life through his name"* (John 20:30-31).

The word of God is also the necessary food for the growth of those who have been born again (1 Pet. 1:22- 2:2). Paul reminded the elders of the church of Ephesus that the word of God is able to build us up and give us an inheritance among those who are sanctified (Acts 20:32). Let us learn from these passages that, for one to be an effective preacher of the gospel, he must use the Scriptures and use them properly. In Paul's second letter to Timothy, he told the young preacher, *"Study to show thyself approved unto God, a workman that needeth not to be ashamed, rightly dividing the word of truth"* (2 Tim. 2:15). The way for all preachers of today to gain the knowledge of the word of God is to study or give diligence. Those who attempt to preach the gospel of Christ without putting forth a diligent effort to know what it says will have reason to be ashamed as workmen. The result of such study by one who is passionate about doing the work of an evangelist will be that God's word will be rightly divided or handled aright. There is much more involved in handling the word of God aright than what appears on the surface. Rightly dividing the word of truth involves an understanding of the difference between the Old Testament and the New Testament, a common mistake among many preachers, and much more. A cardinal rule of Bible study is to recognize who is addressed by the writer in any given passage. One way this is violated is by applying what Jesus said specifically to his apostles to all people. For example, Jesus promised his apostles that he would send the Holy Spirit who would guide them into all truth (John 16:13). Many read this statement and think the Holy Spirit will guide them to an understanding of the truth they could not have without a direct and personal appearance of the Spirit to help them. Effective preachers will give careful attention to what the Bible says as they prepare and present lessons to help others who are seeking salvation.

There is a vast difference in the use of Scripture in the preaching of the first century apostles and evangelists and the preaching being done by many in this generation. The lack of use of the word of God by many preachers today is a reminder of the way it was in the time of Jeremiah. He wrote, *"An astonishing and horrible thing has been committed in the land: the prophets prophesy falsely, and the priests rule by their own power; and My people love to have it so. But what will you do in the end?"* (Jer. 5:30-31). Many preachers now are more interested in preaching what the people want rather than the truth they need. The kind of preaching that entertains and makes the people feel good about themselves without calling upon them to measure up to the standard God has set in his word is the kind being done by the majority.

Paul's charge to Timothy was to *"preach the word"* (2 Tim. 4:2), warning him that the time would come when men would not endure sound doctrine. That time has come and many want their ears tickled rather than their minds challenged with the word of God. God's word makes some uncomfortable because they are not willing to apply it to their own lives, and make the necessary changes to be what he expects of us. Remember that effective preaching accomplishes its goal, which is the salvation of the souls of men. God chose the foolishness of preaching to save them that believe (1 Cor. 1:21). The context of this verse shows that the thing preached must be the true gospel of Jesus Christ. The fables and pleasing stories that characterize much of the preaching being done in this generation will not result in the salvation of the souls of sinful men. In spite of such plain teaching in the Bible most seem to think that the kind of preaching that pleases the most people is the preaching that is most effective.

Chapter Two

He Preached The Gospel, Not With Wisdom of Words

(1 Corinthians 1:17-31)

Some Changes That Took Place When Saul (Paul) Was Converted to Christ

When Saul, of Tarsus, was converted to the Lord some drastic changes took place in his life. He wrote about these changes later, saying, *"I am crucified with Christ: nevertheless I live; yet not I but Christ liveth in me: and the life I now live in the flesh I live by the faith of the Son of God, who loved me, and gave himself for me"* (Gal. 2:20). One of the most notable of these changes had to do with his loyalty. Before his conversion he was persecuting Christ and making havoc of his church, but when the Lord appeared to him and identified himself to Saul he believed in him as God's Son for the rest of his life.

To be an effective preacher today one must have strong abiding faith in Jesus Christ as the Son of the living God. This means that our loyalty must be to him and not to any man or religious group. It is sad but true that this is not the condition that prevails in the religious world of today. Many seem to be more interested in pleasing the people than in knowing what it takes to please God and then doing that. Paul preached as he did because of the faith he had in Jesus (2 Cor. 4:13). Like the twelve apostles he was determined to obey God rather than man (see Acts 5:29). He also knew, as John wrote, that we must be faithful unto death in order to receive the crown of life (Rev. 2:10). Those who are weak in faith are in danger of compromising the truth in order to please certain people, and thereby cease to be effective preachers of God's word.

Saul thought he was doing God service while he was persecuting Christ, but when he realized that what he was doing was wrong he repented. His repentance is indicated by the fact that for three days he neither ate nor drank and prayed until Ananias, the preacher the Lord sent to him, told him what to do. That change brought about a different way of life. Repentance involves a change of one's attitude toward sin and results in a change of the way he lives. Whereas Saul had previously tried to destroy the church Jesus promised to build, he began immediately to preach Jesus as the Christ. His life changed from that of being the persecutor to that of the persecuted.

He Preached the Gospel Not With Wisdom of Words
(1 Cor. 1:17-31)

From the beginning of Christianity preaching has had a prominent place. None has done it better than the apostle Paul, except of course, Jesus the Son of God. Anyone who is concerned about maintaining the purity of Christianity would do well to study what the New Testament has to say about the preaching of this great apostle. This is not to minimize the importance of the work of the other apostles, and others who faithfully labored in preaching the gospel, nor to exalt Paul above what is in keeping with what he deserves as a humble servant of the Lord. An in-depth study of the preaching of Paul will lead one to look earnestly at the content of his message, observe that he always preached what the audience needed, and never wavered from the truth. It is also important to consider the manner in which he preached God's message of salvation. He had a reason for preaching the way he did. This fact will become obvious when we look at some of the Bible passages that deal with why he preached as he did.

Paul asked the brethren at Colossae to pray for him that he may make the mystery manifest as he ought to speak (Col. 4:2-4). He wanted his message to be plain enough for all to understand. Paul felt an indebtedness to preach the gospel to everyone he could, and therefore was ready to preach the gospel in Rome (Rom. 1:14-15). There was a compulsion so strong within him that he wrote,

"For though I preach the gospel, I have nothing to glory of: for necessity is laid upon me: yea, woe is unto me, if I preach not the gospel" (1 Cor. 9:16). Paul did not hesitate to take advantage to preach the gospel at every opportunity, and neither should we.

Paul Sent to Preach the Gospel

Paul went from Athens to Corinth to preach the gospel. When he arrived he met Aquila, with his wife, Priscilla, who were tentmakers, as was Paul. Because they were of the same trade he abode with them, and as his custom was, he went to the synagogue where he reasoned and persuaded the Jews and Greeks. Subsequently Silas and Timothy came. Paul then testified to the Jews that Jesus was Christ. Their opposition to the truth did not deter Paul from continuing to preach the gospel, but he turned to the Gentiles who were more receptive to the word of God. Paul remained there a year and six months, longer than in most places. We know from the fact Paul wrote two letters to the church of God at Corinth that his preaching was effective among those who honestly considered what he had to say.

In the first letter he wrote to the church there, he reminded them of the preaching he did and why he preached as he did. Using a Hebrew idiom which put the emphasis on the preaching of the gospel, and with which the people then were familiar, he told them God did not send him to baptize but to preach the gospel (1 Cor. 1:17). One is not to conclude from this that Paul considered baptism unnecessary, for he did baptize some, Crispus and Gaius being among them (1 Cor. 1:14). He himself was told to be baptized to wash away his sins (Acts 22:16) which he did (see Rom. 6:3). Though Paul was an educated man, and no doubt well able to use such wisdom of words characteristic of the philosophers of that day, he did not want the people to be persuaded by such polished rhetoric, but with the simple message of the crucifixion of Jesus Christ on the cross. Effective preaching of the gospel depends upon the power of the truth of it received in the hearts of the believers, and not upon the power of argumentation and the beauty of the eloquence of men.

The Preaching of the Cross
Involves Preaching the Historical Fact of the Crucifixion

The reason Paul gave for preaching the gospel: not with wisdom of words was *"lest the cross of Christ should be made of none effect"* (1 Cor. 1:17). The cross is used frequently in Scripture to refer to the crucifixion of Christ and all that is involved in the significance of that event. Therefore the preaching of the cross involves the preaching of the historical fact of the crucifixion of Christ. The fact that Jesus was crucified on the cross is of no value to those who deny that his death was for our sins. Stating the facts and presenting evidence to prove them as Paul did is God's plan to save our souls. Jesus claimed to be the Son of God and proved his claim, pointing to his own crucifixion and resurrection which he said he did voluntarily (John 10:17-18). Yet many rejected him before and after his crucifixion. Various sins were committed by those who cried out for his crucifixion, and many today are guilty of these same sins.

Blinded by tradition the religious leaders of that day could not accept that which differed from their former beliefs. The same is true among many today who are so bound by tradition they cannot see the necessity of obeying the gospel in order to be saved from their sins. There was also a materialistic attitude that showed such interest in the profit from the traffic in the temple courts they would not allow anything to happen that would disturb that. Through the years there have been those who show more interest in the money they receive for their preaching than passion for lost souls. Jesus condemned this as he pointed out they were making his Father's house a house of merchandise (John 2:16). Some are politically motivated, and rather than causing a tumult, they, like Pilate, try to wash their hands of the matter and occupy a neutral position, unwilling to pay the price and stand up for Jesus (Matt. 27:24). The emotionalism of the crowd, stirred up by the mob to do what they did not understand, influences many today. Then there is the traitor who professes to be a friend, but his selfish interest causes him to betray Jesus. Judas did that. Those who were guilty of these and other sins combined forces and committed the most heinous crime ever carried out by mankind when they crucified the sinless Son of God. To be motivated by these or any other ulterior considerations is to cheapen the gospel and put one's soul in jeopardy.

Involves Preaching the Means God Chose to Redeem Man
Preaching of the cross involves preaching it as the means

God chose to redeem man. Jesus, who knew no sin, was made to be sin for us, that we might be reconciled to God, and that we might be made the righteousness of God in him (2 Cor. 5:18-21). Reconciliation is the process of restoring a relationship that had been severed. In this case man by his sins severed himself from God and therefore was in need of being reconciled to God. This passage teaches that God is the One who reconciles certain ones to himself and that reconciliation is in Christ. The gospel preached by the apostles, Paul included, is the word of reconciliation. Jesus gave himself for us that he might redeem us from all iniquity (Tit. 2:14). He suffered for our sins that he might bring us to God (1 Pet. 3:18), and redeemed us to God by his blood (Rev. 5:9).

Only through the redemption that is in Christ Jesus could man be declared righteous and God be both just and the justifier of them that believe in Jesus. This fact is stated and discussed by Paul in the Roman letter. The righteousness of God, i.e. the way man may be counted righteous or justified in the sight of God, is revealed in the gospel, and offered to believers (Rom. 1:16, 17; 3:22). Elsewhere we learn that the gospel is given to produce faith (Phil. 3:8-9). Redemption has to do with a deliverance brought about by a ransom having been paid (Matt. 20:28; Eph. 1:7; 1 Pet. 1:18-19). To make this possible God set forth Christ to be a propitiation for our sins which has to do with a means whereby sin is covered or remitted. The word originally had reference to the cover or lid of the ark, but also refers to Christ, who through his death is the personal means by whom God shows the mercy of his justifying grace to the sinner who believes (Vine's *Expository Dictionary of Biblical Words*).

To understand the teaching set forth in Romans 3:23-26 one needs to observe the punctuation, especially in verse 25. There are two modifying phrases to the word "propitiation." "Through faith" is the means by which the propitiation is received and becomes effective. "In his blood" indicates Christ as the sacrificial offering. The offering has been made and is available to all, but it is effective only to those who believe, hence there is no reconciliation except for those who believe. God could be just in dealing with sin and at the same time forgive those who were penitent in view of what was to take place when Jesus was crucified. He redeemed us from the curse of the law, being made a curse for us (Gal. 3:13). He was made to be sin for us, treated as though he was a sinner, but he knew no sin. He did this for us that we might be made the righteousness of God in him (2 Cor. 5:21). His death was for the redemption of the transgressions that were under the first testament as well as for us (Heb. 9:15). The believers under consideration in these passages are obedient believers, which is clearly stated (Rom. 16:26).

Involves Preaching Its Transforming Power in Our Lives

It was in the resurrection that the transforming power of the cross became real and effective. Early in his public ministry Jesus told the Jews, *"Destroy this temple, and in three days I will raise it up"* (John 2:19). They did not understand what Jesus was talking about at the time, but when he was raised from the dead his disciples remembered what he had said unto them, and believed the Scriptures and what Jesus had said. The disciples, who witnessed the resurrection and realized what it meant to them, went out to tell others of it. The apostles were commanded by the Lord to preach it (Mark 16:15), which they did beginning in Jerusalem on the first Pentecost after the resurrection of Jesus (Acts 2:1-4). After that, they and other disciples preached to others, even suffering for so doing (Acts 5:41; 8:1-5). The cross had such an impact upon the apostle Paul that he said, *"But God forbid that I should glory, save in the cross of our Lord Jesus Christ, by whom the world is crucified unto me, and I unto the world"* (Gal. 6:14). In view of this it is sad when there are professed Christians to whom the cross has no real transforming power. Instead of being transformed by the renewing of their minds, many continue in the same mind set as before, allowing such things as the cares of this world and the deceitfulness of riches to choke out the word. On the other hand those who are transformed by the preaching of the cross will let the word of Christ dwell in them richly and order their every thought, word, and deed.

Classes of Those to Whom Paul Preached: Them That Perish

The preaching of the cross is foolishness to them. The cross of Christ was a stumbling block to the Jews which they could not get over because they were looking for a king who would rule with great pomp and regal power. They would not have one for their ruler who died such an accursed death, a manner of death usually reserved for the worst kind of criminals. They were seeking for a sign but rejected the plain signs that were given. Peter reminded them on the day of Pentecost that Jesus was a man approved of God among them by miracles, wonders, and signs which God did by him in their midst, as they knew (Acts 2:22). There are still those who are not persuaded by the testimony of the Scriptures, and are looking for signs as the Jews did in the first century.

The Greeks sought after wisdom, and the preaching of the cross was foolishness to them. They were men who prided themselves in their achievements in the arts and sciences, and the idea of one becoming a leader and savior by going to a cross was repugnant to them. It seems there are those in every generation who are perishing because they see nothing in the death of Jesus on the cross to do them any good. Those who would preach effectively as Paul did must point out these facts to their hearers.

Those Who Are Being Saved

To those who are saved the gospel is the power of God. Jesus had said earlier, referring to the death that he would die, that if he were lifted up he would draw all men to himself (John 12:32-33). It is by the cross that man has the opportunity to be reconciled to God. When man sins he makes himself an enemy of God, separating himself from God as Isaiah wrote, *". . .your iniquities have separated between you and your God, and your sins have hid his face from you, that he will not hear"* (Isa. 59:2). But God loves us, and even while we were his enemies he sent his Son to die for us that we might be reconciled to him by the cross. Paul wrote to the saints at Rome that we were reconciled to God by the death of his Son and that we shall be saved by his life (Rom. 5:8-10). He wrote to the Ephesians that both Jews and Gentiles might be reconciled to God in one body by the cross (Eph. 2:14-16). The word of reconciliation was committed to the apostles, who, as ambassadors for Christ, prayed that the people might be reconciled to God (2 Cor. 5:18-21). It is no wonder then that Paul was so concerned that the preaching of the cross not be camouflaged, disguised, muffled, or concealed by the wisdom of words of men, but presented in plain and convincing language so his hearers could understand. The lesson is no less important for those who would be soul winners for Christ today.

Why God Chose This Plan:
That No Flesh Should Glory Before God

The attitude of many seems to be that they are self-sufficient, and need no help from anyone to do whatever they want to do. This is a dangerous attitude regardless of what the endeavor might be. With regard to the salvation of the soul, the Bible teaches us that it is not by our own achievements (works of righteousness we have done) that we are saved but according to God's mercy (Tit. 3:5). In case of a failure the greater the value of that which is lost, the greater the tragedy. In view of the value the Lord places upon the soul (Matt. 16:26), we should do all we can to make our calling and election sure. Our dependence upon the Lord for our salvation clearly shows that the wise man will not be saved because of his wisdom, or the noble man because of his high birth, or the rich man because of his wealth. Jeremiah wrote, *"Thus saith the Lord, Let not the wise man glory in his wisdom, neither let the mighty man glory in his might, let not the rich man glory in his riches: But let him that glorieth glory in this, that he understandeth and knoweth me, that I am the Lord which exercise lovingkindness, judgment, and righteousness, in the earth: for in these things I delight, saith the Lord."* (Jer. 9:23-24). Paul wrote that we should glory in the cross of our Lord Jesus Christ (Gal. 6:14).

The humble who recognize their own sinfulness and willingly submit to the Lord are those who will hear and understand. The publican who recognized he was a sinner went down to his house justified whereas the self righteous Pharisee did not (Luke 18:9-14). Jesus spoke of some in whom a prophecy of Isaiah was fulfilled. They heard, but did not understand, they saw but did not perceive because they stopped their own ears and closed their eyes. Therefore they were not converted, and the Lord did not heal them (Matt. 13:14-16). No one, then or now, could conclude from the preaching Paul did that they had reason to expect the Lord to save them because of their own deeds. Is that the kind of preaching being done by the majority of preachers today?

The message of the cross leaves no man exactly as it found him. A radical change takes place in the lives of all who receive the preaching of the cross and act upon it. As the same sun melts wax and hardens clay, so the same message pricks the heart of the sensitive and hardens the heart of the impenitent. Paul's statement to the Corinthians, *". . .To the one we are the savor of death unto death; and to the other the savor of life unto life"* (2 Cor. 2:16), has reference to the work of Paul in preaching the gospel, which condemned the unbelieving and strengthened those who believed. There were those who lived in the time of Paul who corrupted the word of God, which Paul did not do. For preaching to be effective today as Paul's was, it must be done as of sincerity, not corrupting the word of God as some do.

Chapter Three

He Preached in Demonstration of the Spirit and of Power

(1 Corinthians 2:1-5)

Effective preaching as Paul did it requires that we exercise extreme care as to the source of our information as well as the manner of presentation. Paul's statement in the first part of the second chapter of the first Corinthian letter is a continuation of the subject he began in chapter one. Paul was familiar with the way both Jews and Greeks used excellency of speech and words of wisdom and was determined not to be guilty of doing the same. He reminded them that he came declaring the testimony of God and was determined not to know anything among them, save Jesus Christ, and him crucified.

The Subject Matter of Paul's Preaching:
Jesus Christ and Him Crucified

Paul's own statement, *"For I determined not to know any thing among you, save Jesus Christ, and him crucified,"* tells us that Jesus Christ was the central theme of Paul's preaching. But what is involved in that kind of preaching? Some attention was given in chapter two of this book to the cross of Christ, but there is more involved in preaching Jesus Christ.

Paul Preached the Person of Jesus. The name "Jesus" means Savior or Deliverer and refers to the person of Jesus. The angel announced to Joseph before Jesus was born that Mary was with child of the Holy Spirit and that she would bare a son and he should call his name Jesus: for he would save his people from their sins (Matt. 1:21). This helps us to understand the statement of Paul in the second Corinthian letter when he wrote, *"For we preach not ourselves, but Christ Jesus the Lord: and ourselves your servants for Jesus' sake"* (2 Cor. 4:5). Therefore, when we believe in Jesus Christ, we believe in a person, a Divine person, and not in simply a set of rules.

This involves preaching Christ as both subject and fulfillment of prophecy. Isaiah prophesied that a virgin would conceive and bare a son (Isa. 7:14) and that the government would be upon his shoulder, and that his name would be called Wonderful, Counselor, Mighty God, Everlasting Father, Prince of Peace" (Isa. 9:6). Preaching what the Bible tells about the person of Jesus of necessity includes telling that he was in the beginning with God and that he was God, as well as the fact that he became flesh and dwelt among men (John 1:1-4, 14).

Paul Preached the Office of Christ. The office of Christ was unique to him, and has reference to him as the Messiah, which is the word that describes this position of him in the Old Testament. The literal meaning of this word is "the anointed one." During the Old Testament days prophets, priests, and kings were anointed.

God told Moses that Aaron and his sons were to minister to him as priests. Detailed information was given concerning their preparation for this office. Included in these instructions was this, *". . .and shalt anoint them, and consecrate them, and sanctify them, that they may minister unto me in the priest's office"* (Exod. 28:41b). Further instructions are given in chapters 29 and 30. The Lord sent Samuel to anoint Saul to be king over his people, Israel, which he did, charging him to hearken unto the voice of the words of the Lord (1 Sam. 15:1). Elijah was told by the Lord to anoint Elisha to be prophet in his room (1 Kings 19:16). In each of these the thought of consecrating or setting apart to a special office or work was prominent.

It is interesting to note that in the Old Testament period some were anointed to two of these positions, but none to all three. Aaron was a prophet (Exod. 7:1) and priest (Exod. 28:1). Melchisedec was king of Salem and priest of the most high God (Heb. 7:1);

David was anointed as king (2 Sam. 2:4) and a prophet (Acts 2:30). Jesus is our prophet (Deut. 18:15, 18, 19; Acts 2:22-23), priest (Heb. 3:1; 4:15; 7:25), and king (Acts 2:30). Effectively preaching Christ as Paul did includes informing the people that, as prophet, Jesus has said enough to save all men. His words are Spirit and they are life (John 6:63), and there is no other to whom we can go if we reject him (John 6:68). As priest he has done enough in offering himself as our sacrifice, and in making intercession for us, to save us from sin. The Hebrew writer tells us that he is able to save to the uttermost all who come unto God by him, seeing he ever lives to make intercession for us (Heb. 7:25), and if we reject him there is no more sacrifice for sin (Heb. 10:26). As king he is powerful enough to save all who will come to him in faith, obeying his every command. He is king of kings and Lord of lords, who only has immortality (1 Tim. 6:15-16), and there is no escape for those who forsake the great salvation which was first spoken by the Lord (Heb. 2:3).

Paul Preached Christ Jesus the Lord. Though it is not mentioned in this passage of Scripture, it is said elsewhere that Paul preached Christ Jesus the Lord (2 Cor. 4:5). The word "lord" that has reference to one who is owner of a person or property is properly applied to the Messiah who by his death and resurrection purchased a special people. It is he who is the one Lord Jesus Christ, by whom are all things (1 Cor. 8:6). In order to be saved from our sins it is necessary that we confess him as Lord (Rom. 10:9, 10), but simply calling him "Lord, Lord," is not enough. Jesus asked this question of some, *"And why call ye me, Lord, Lord, and do not the things which I say?"* (Luke 6:46). Jesus also said, *"Not every one that saith unto me, Lord, Lord, shall enter into the kingdom of heaven; but he that doeth the will of my Father which is in heaven"* (Matt. 7:21). Since the time will come when every knee shall bow at his name and every tongue shall confess that Jesus Christ is Lord (Phil. 2:9-11), then effective preaching must include preaching him as Lord.

Paul Preached Christ Crucified. In the prophecy of David the manner of death is presented as by crucifixion, when he said, *"they pierced my hands and my feet"* (Ps. 22:16). The entire fifty-third chapter of Isaiah tells of the suffering he would endure which was necessary for him to fulfill his purpose of saving sinful man. He told his disciples that he must suffer many things and be killed, but they did not understand (Matt. 16:21; 20:28). He was made perfect through suffering, and in doing so was able to bring many sons to glory (Heb. 2:10). The crucifixion was a necessary part of the good news of the gospel by which we are saved, if we keep in memory what the apostles preached (1 Cor. 15:1-4).

This Was the Testimony of God

God gave testimony that Jesus was the Christ on more than one occasion. To the Jews at Jerusalem Jesus said, *"But I have greater witness than that of John: for the works which the Father hath given me to finish, the same works that I do, bear witness of me, that the Father hath sent me. And the Father Himself, which hath sent me, hath borne witness of me. Ye have neither heard His voice at any time, nor seen his shape"* (John 5:36-37).

God also gave testimony that Jesus is the Christ to Peter and the other apostles at Caesarea Philippi. Peter confessed that he was the Christ the Son of God, and Jesus told him that this was not revealed to him by flesh and blood, but the Father in heaven had revealed it to him (Matt. 16:13-18). Therefore we conclude that what Paul preached was what he received by Divine revelation.

The Manner of Paul's Preaching Christ:

Negatively

Paul reminded his brethren in Corinth concerning the manner in which he came to them preaching Christ that he *"came not with excellency of speech or of wisdom"* (1 Cor. 2:1). He did not want them to think he came with a feeling of excellency or superiority over them. In preaching Christ crucified, Paul was not concerned with brilliant sentence structure or beautiful rhetoric. The theme of Christ was independent of such, and indeed too great for it. How can one presume to think he can improve on the plain and powerful word of God by the use of his wisdom of speech? One may as well try to improve on the beauty of a rose bush in full bloom.

Paul also reminded them that his preaching was *"not with enticing words of man's wisdom"* (1 Cor. 2:4). His speech (probably referring primarily to his discourse on doctrine), and preaching (his public proclamation of facts), were not presented with the keen dialect of the philosophers or with human eloquence. Paul's purpose in preaching was not to entertain such as many today seem to think is necessary. He did not use the flowery speech calculated to captivate the ear, but that which would convict and instruct his audience in righteousness.

This is in keeping with what he told Timothy when he charged him to *"preach the word"* (2 Tim. 4:2). Effective preaching during that period of time included reproving, rebuking, and exhorting with all long suffering and doctrine, using words of truth and soberness as Paul did when he appeared before Agrippa (Acts 26:25). The Holy Spirit did not inspire Paul to write this exclusively for Timothy's benefit, but for all in every age who would be effective in presenting God's saving message to a lost world.

Positively

Paul described the way he conducted himself while he was with them in this way. He told them he was with them in weakness. It is not clear whether or not Paul was referring to his physical weaknesses which he mentioned in his second letter to the church at Corinth, *"For his letters, say they, are weighty and powerful; but his bodily presence is weak, and his speech contemptible"* (2 Cor. 10:10). In his letter to the churches of Galatia he wrote, *"Ye know how through infirmity of the flesh I preached the gospel unto you at the first"* (Gal. 4:13). This great man did not consider himself to be behind the chiefest apostles in anything (2 Cor. 12:11), even though he was deeply conscious of his own insufficiency in comparison to the magnitude of his work. This should be a great reminder to all of us of our dependence upon the Lord for help as we engage in such important work. Paul acknowledged that his help came from God before and during his imprisonment for the cause of Christ (Acts 26:22; 2 Tim. 4:17).

Paul was also with them in fear. He was not moved by fear of bonds or afflictions which awaited him in Jerusalem, but probably by fear brought about by the sense of the great desire he had to fulfill all the Lord had for him to do. The word "fear" in this passage has to do with the reverence and awe one has for the all powerful God. It is the same word used by the writer to persuade men in view of the judgment of Christ which all must face (2 Cor. 5:10-11). No doubt Paul had learned the lesson Jesus taught when he said, *"And fear not them which kill the body, but are not able to kill the soul: but rather fear him which is able to destroy both soul and body in hell"* (Matt. 10:28). Effective preaching as Paul did it is an awesome responsibility, and none should be moved by persecution, popularity, or pressure from within or without to fail in their efforts to finish their course. Careful advanced preparation and a feeling of apprehension lest we make mistakes and thereby lead someone astray will help accomplish this. Familiarity with and dependence upon the word of God which can only come by a will to do God's will is essential in dealing with fear in the proper manner

The Scripture also tells us that he was with them in much trembling. It was not the fact he was appointed a preacher, an apostle, and a teacher of the Gentiles nor the gospel which he preached that caused this trembling, for Paul was ashamed of neither (see 2 Tim. 1:12 and Rom. 1:16). Nor was it because of any personal harm or danger that Paul trembled, for he was in nothing terrified by his adversaries (Phil. 1:28). Paul's statement that he was with the Corinthians in weakness, fear, and much trembling had primary reference to the manner in which he conducted himself while in their presence. He also said that his speech was *"in demonstration of the Spirit and of power"* (1 Cor. 2:4), before he tells them why he preached in that way. What Paul preached he received by revelation of the Spirit, and used the words that the Spirit taught to convey the message to his hearers. This was true in his speech and his preaching; not only to the Corinthians, but everywhere he went. He wrote to the Galatians that what he preached to them he neither received from man, nor was he taught it, but it came to him by revelation of Jesus Christ (Gal. 1:12), and to the Ephesians that the mystery which in times past was not made known to the sons of men, was then revealed to his holy apostles and prophets by the Spirit (Eph. 3:5). This harmonized with the promise the Lord made to the twelve apostles earlier. He said he would send the Holy Spirit upon them and that he would guide them into all truth (John 16:13).

Other Scriptures help us understand more fully what Paul meant by saying he came to them in power. The apostles had been given power to work miracles to confirm the word that they preached (Mark 16:19-20). The Lord fulfilled this promise. On the first Pentecost following the resurrection and ascension of the Lord, the Holy Spirit came upon the apostles and they began to speak with other tongues as the Spirit gave them utterance (Acts 2:1-4). The writer of Hebrews tells us that the great salvation was first spoken by the Lord, and was confirmed by those who heard him and that God bore witness with signs and wonders, divers miracles, and gifts of the Holy Spirit, according to his own will (Heb. 2:1-4).

The power with which he came to them was vested in the gospel, the word of God, which is declared to be the power of God unto salvation unto all those who believe (Rom. 1:16). This same writer also wrote to the Thessalonians commending them for the manner in which they received the word of God, which he said worked effectually in those who believe it (1 Thess. 2:13). The word of God is said to be quick (living) and powerful, sharper than a two edged sword (Heb. 4:12).

The Reason Paul Preached This Way:

"That Your Faith Should Not Stand in the Wisdom of Men, But in the Power of God"

Without question Paul wanted his readers to understand that his preaching was from God and not man. The message he preached was revealed to him by the Holy Spirit (1 Cor. 2:10). He wrote to the churches of Galatia that he did not receive his message from man and neither was he taught it by man, but that it came by revelation (Gal. 1:11, 12). His message was the same as that preached by the Twelve on the first Pentecost following the resurrection who spoke as the Spirit gave them utterance (Acts 2:1-4).

It is important for all to understand that faith is essential for our salvation. It is also important to know the source of that saving faith. In his preaching Paul affirmed that to be the word of God. We learn from the letter to the saints at Rome that faith comes by hearing the word of God (Rom. 10:17). John wrote the same thing as he told about some of the things that Jesus did. He said they were written that we might believe that Jesus Christ is the Son of God; and that believing we might have life through his name (John 20:30, 31). The faith that saves from sin and provides a sure foundation for stability in times of trials and tribulations must be on solid ground. Too many today have their faith based on the imagination, eloquence, or learning of their favorite preacher, upon the authority of the church, or upon their own opinions, none of which will produce the saving faith mentioned in the Bible. This is the kind of faith each individual must have in order to obey from the heart that form of doctrine which was delivered by inspired apostles at which time we are made free from sin (Rom. 6:17-18). We urge each reader to consider this very carefully, and make sure you have faith that is based upon the word of God and that will motivate you to obey the Lord that you might be saved.

Chapter Four

He Taught the Same Thing in Every Church

(1 Corinthians 4:17; 7:17; 16:1; 1:10)

There are preachers who will change their message to suit the audience to whom they are preaching. This was not true of the apostle Paul. He wrote to the church in Corinth telling them he sent Timothy to bring them in remembrance of his ways in Christ, as he taught everywhere in every church (1 Cor. 4:17). Paul's teaching and practice were the same in every church, and he was neither ashamed nor afraid for the Corinthians to know how he conducted himself before all men. Reading through the New Testament Scriptures one cannot help but be impressed with the fact that all the apostles and other inspired evangelists of the first century preached the same thing Paul did. What about preachers of today, are all of them preaching the same thing Paul preached? In view of the many differing religious groups that now exist the answer to this question should be obvious. Considering the fact that God wants his people to believe and practice the same thing makes the significance of this statement clear to all who believe the Bible to be the inspired word of God.

Paul's Preaching the Same Thing in Every Church Indicates Unity of Doctrine

The Scriptures teach oneness of doctrine. Not only did Paul preach the same thing in every church, but all the apostles and other inspired men of the first century preached the same thing

Paul did. How can we account for the fact that they all preached the same thing? The answer should be easy when we consider the fact they were all guided by the same Holy Spirit of God as Jesus promised (John 16:13). In this way we can account for the oneness of doctrine that characterized the preaching of the inspired preachers of that time. Every time in the Bible reference is made to the teaching of these men, the singular form of the word "doctrine" is used. An example of this is Paul's statement to Timothy in the first letter he wrote to him. He said, *"As I besought thee to abide still at Ephesus, when I went into Macedonia, that thou mightest charge some that they teach no other **doctrine**"* (1 Tim. 1:3). In contrast to this the Bible uses the plural "doctrines" when reference is made to the teachings of men. Jesus said, *"But in vain they do worship me, teaching for **doctrines** the commandments of men"* (Matt. 15:9). The way we can know whether all are preaching the same thing today is by comparing what they say with the New Testament, God's final and complete revelation to man (2 Tim. 3:16-17).

The Lord, through one of his inspired apostles, has pronounced a curse on all who preach another gospel. This is what the apostle Paul was inspired to write on this subject. *"But though we, or an angel from heaven, preach any other gospel unto you than that which we have preached unto you, let him be accursed. As we said before, so say I now again, If any man preach any other gospel unto you than that ye have received, let him be accursed"* (Gal. 1:8, 9). In spite of all the warnings in the word of God against teaching anything other than what the apostles taught as they were guided by the Holy Spirit there are many who think it doesn't make any difference what one teaches or believes just so he is honest and sincere.

Paul also wrote to the church at Corinth telling them that they should all speak the same thing, and that there should be no divisions among them (1 Cor. 1:10). This point is punctuated and emphasized in a letter the apostle John wrote. He said, *"Whosoever transgresseth, and abideth not in the doctrine of Christ, hath not God. He that abideth in the doctrine of Christ, he hath both the Father and the Son"* (2 John 9).

The Scriptures teach that the requirements for salvation

are the same for everyone. The conditions Jesus gave for salvation when he told his disciples to go preach to every creature are the same that Paul obeyed and that he taught others. Jesus commissioned his disciples to preach the gospel to every creature, and that he that believes and is baptized shall be saved (Mark 16:15-16). There is a record of this same commission found in Matthew 28:18-20 and Luke 24:46-49 where repentance is also mentioned as a condition of salvation. All the conditions Jesus gave for our salvation are found in these three passages of Scripture. We must obey all of them in order to receive the blessings the Lord promised.

On the day of Pentecost after Jesus ascended back to the Father the apostles began preaching as the Lord had told them as they were guided by the Holy Spirit. Those who heard them preach that day were Jews from every nation under heaven. When they heard about the crucifixion and resurrection of Jesus Christ and were called upon to know assuredly that God had made him both Lord and Christ, they wanted to know what to do. Since they already believed, they were told to repent and be baptized for the remission of their sins (Acts 2:38). That was exactly what Jesus had told the apostles earlier to preach.

The conditions for salvation for those who were not Jews was the same. Jesus not only told these men what they were to preach, but gave the plan to carry it to the whole world. He said they were to begin in Jerusalem, then to all Judea, then to Samaria, and then to the uttermost part of the earth (Acts 1:8). After preaching the gospel in Jerusalem for a while there were those disciples of the Lord who went to all the regions of Judea (Acts 8:1-4). Soon after that we are told that Philip went to Samaria and preached Christ. We are told what was involved in preaching Christ in Acts 8:12 which says, *"But when they believed Philip preaching the things concerning the kingdom of God, and the name of Jesus Christ, they were baptized, both men and women."* This tells us that the conditions for the Samaritans were the same as they were for the Jews. Peter told Cornelius, the first Gentile to be converted, the same thing when he was sent to preach to him. A record of this is found in Acts chapters ten and eleven. Note especially Acts 10:48 where we learn that Peter commanded them to be baptized.

The Bible tells us what Paul (formerly known as Saul) did in order to have his past sins forgiven. He was on the road to Damascus to bind any who were followers of Christ, and take them to Jerusalem that they might be further punished for their faith when a bright light shined down from heaven and he fell to the ground blind. A voice spoke to him and he asked who it was. He was told it was the Lord whom he had been persecuting, and it made him tremble. He asked the Lord what he would have him do. The Lord told him to go into the city and it would be told him what he must do. The Lord told him the man's name who would tell him. Saul did as he was instructed and there Ananias came to him and told him what to do (Acts 9:1-18). Paul told some Roman officials about what happened, and said that Ananias said to him, *"And now why tarriest thou? Arise, and be baptized, and wash away thy sins, calling on the name of the Lord"* (Acts 22:16). He affirmed that he was baptized into Christ in the letter he wrote to the saints in Rome (Rom. 6:3).

What did Paul teach the people of Ephesus about how they were saved? In a letter he wrote to them he said *"For by grace are ye saved through faith; and not of yourselves: it is the gift of God: Not of works, lest any man should boast"* (Eph. 2:8-9). Does this statement contradict what Paul did and what he taught others to do that they may receive the salvation that is in Christ Jesus? Certainly not as we shall see when we consider this passage further. To understand his teaching in this statement we must consider what he taught about how we are saved by grace, and what faith has to do with bringing about our salvation. How do the grace of God and the faith of man come together and result in man's salvation? I think it would be safe to say that virtually everyone who believes that Jesus Christ is the Son of God believes we are saved by the grace of God. There are differences, however, about whether salvation by grace is conditional or unconditional. If it were unconditional then all would be saved, for the grace of God is extended to all. If, on the other hand, it is conditional then it behooves us to study the Scriptures and learn what the conditions are. Let us look at this and some related passages in the Bible to find the answer. To learn the truth on this subject one must understand that the grace of God has to do with the unmerited favor he bestows upon us, favor we do not deserve.

That salvation by grace is conditional is clearly taught in the Bible. Both God and man have something to do in bringing about one's salvation. Grace is God's part and faith is man's part. Paul wrote, *"For the grace of God that bringeth salvation hath appeared to all men, teaching us that, denying ungodliness and worldly lusts, we should live soberly, righteously, and godly, in this present world"* (Tit. 2:11-12). The writer of the book of Hebrews tells us that it was *"by the grace of God"* that Jesus tasted death for every man. Since not every one will be saved (Matt. 25:46), the grace of God must be conditional and there is something for man to do that he might enjoy the blessings of God's grace. This passage of Scripture expresses what that is by saying it is *"through faith."* This does not have reference to a dead, inactive faith, but a living, active, obedient faith. The record of the many who accomplished great things by faith when they did what God required of them clearly teaches this (Heb. 11). Two of these examples should suffice to make this point: *"By faith Noah, . . .prepared an ark to the saving of his house"* (v. 7), and *"By faith Abraham, . . .obeyed"* (v. 8). The Bible teaches that we must do the will of the Father in heaven in order to enter the kingdom (Matt. 7:21). This lesson is made strong and plain in James 2:24. He wrote, *"Ye see then how that by works a man is justified, and not by faith only"* (Jas. 2:24).

Many of those who teach the doctrine of salvation by faith only rely heavily on this statement of Jesus, *"For God so loved the world, that he gave his only begotten Son, that whosoever believeth in him should not perish, but have everlasting life"* (John 3:16). Some will say that this is all we need in order to learn what to do to be saved. Those who hold this view with whom I have talked agree that we are saved by the grace of God, but grace is not mentioned in this verse. They also say that repentance is necessary on our part, but repentance is not mentioned in this verse. We could go on and on with this list showing that there are other conditions given in the word of God that we must meet in order to receive the salvation offered by a loving Father, but this should suffice to make the point. The truth is that we must submit to all the Lord requires or suffer the consequences. This verse does not contain all that Jesus said about what one must do to have everlasting life. Remember he said, *"He that believeth and is baptized shall be saved; he that believeth not shall be damned"* (Mark 16:16). Does it not seem that the proponents of the doctrine of salvation by faith only are trying to do away with what Jesus and his inspired apostles taught about the necessity of baptism? Paul was effective in winning souls to Christ because he taught what Jesus said. Those who would promise salvation to anyone on anything less than, more than, or different from what Jesus required jeopardize their own souls and the souls of those whom they teach.

Not only did Paul do what the Lord required of him for salvation, but also he taught others to do the same thing wherever he preached the gospel of Jesus Christ. He made a number of trips and preached in many different places, but he never changed his message to accommodate his audience. This is verified by what happened when he preached to some women outside the city of Philippi. Lydia, one of those women, and her household were baptized after hearing Paul preach. The jailer in Philippi also heard Paul preach later and was baptized the same hour of the night. These examples are found in Acts 16. Effective preaching as Paul did it demands that we preach the same thing everywhere we go declaring the message of salvation, and it requires that we preach what Paul and the other inspired men preached.

Paul also preached the same plan of worship. Paul knew the importance of worshiping God according to his revealed will. He wrote to the saints at Philippi, *"For we are the circumcision, which* **worship** *God in the spirit, and rejoice in Christ Jesus, and have no confidence in the flesh"* (Phil. 3:3). On one occasion he remained in Troas for seven days and came together with the disciples on the first day of the week to break bread (eat the Lord's supper). Christians today should follow that example and come together the first day of every week to eat the Lord's supper.

The church at Corinth needed some instructions about the proper way to eat the Lord's supper, and Paul wrote to them about it. Among the things he wrote to them on this subject was that it is a communion with the Lord's body (the bread), and his blood (the fruit of the vine) (1 Cor. 10:16-17). He also wrote to them that it is not for the purpose of satisfying one's appetite, nor is it a social event (1 Cor. 11:20-30). He reminded them that he received of the Lord what he wrote to them, and that, if we eat and drink in an unworthy manner, we eat and drink damnation to our souls. This teaching was not only for the church of God at Corinth, but for all that in every place who call upon the name of Jesus Christ (1 Cor. 1:2).

Paul also taught the same thing everywhere on the matter of worshiping God in song. He wrote that we are to sing with the spirit and with the understanding also (1 Cor. 14:15). He wrote to the Ephesians and the Colossians that we are to sing and make melody in our hearts to the Lord, and that we are to sing with grace in our hearts to the Lord (Eph. 5:19; Col. 3:16). Other writers of the New Testament mention worshiping God in song, but it is significant that no authority is found in the New Testament for using a mechanical instrument to accompany our singing in worship to God. Not only did Paul teach the same thing about singing as worship to God, but all the others taught the same thing also.

Giving of our means is an act of worship in which Christians are to engage. Paul taught on this subject, and he taught the same thing in every church. We know for sure that he gave the same orders on this matter to the church at Corinth, and also to the churches of Galatia (1 Cor. 16:1-2). What he said was that everyone was to lay by him in store upon the first day of the week as God prospered him. The attitude one is to have toward his giving is found in the second letter Paul wrote to this same church in Corinth. Giving is to be done as one purposes in his heart, not grudgingly, or of necessity, for God loves a cheerful giver (2 Cor. 9:7). To be effective in teaching on this unpopular subject, one must give instructions as to the way God says we are to give, the effect it will have upon the one who gives in this way, and that the gifts are to be used to accomplish the purpose God has in mind, not our own selfish interests. It is also important to note that the only way God authorizes his people to raise money to accomplish the work he has given them to do in their collective work is by giving as he has prospered us and to do it on the first day of the week. This would eliminate such things as many are doing to raise money for their projects today—things like collecting and selling all kinds of merchandise, pie suppers, hiring of professional entertainers, and many other methods that are not authorized in the Bible.

Paul taught that every church is to have the same plan of organization. As he and Barnabas were returning to Antioch after preaching in many places, it is said that they ordained elders in every church (Acts 14:23). In later years he was on another journey and called for the elders of the church of Ephesus to meet him on the island of Miletus (Acts 20:17). Among the things he said to them was, *"Take heed therefore unto yourselves, and to all the flock, over the which the Holy Ghost hath made you overseers, to feed the church of God, which he hath purchased with his own blood"* (Acts 20:28). Note that the same group of men are referred to as both elders and bishops. This is clear evidence that those men who have the responsibility of overseeing the flock of God among them are called by different names to indicate different things about who they are and what their work is in the Lord's church. Peter wrote that these men are to tend the flock of God among them which teaches that their oversight is limited to the local church where they were appointed (1 Pet. 5:1-3). These Scriptures show clearly that the responsibility of elders is to oversee the Christians who make up the local congregation over which they serve as bishops. They also teach there are limitations to that oversight—the flock of God among them. When elders extend their oversight to include anything other than the flock of God among them they are not following the teaching Paul did in every church where he went.

This teaching of Paul concerning elders in every church shows that God has revealed a plan for local churches to have organization. The word "church" is some times used in a universal sense to refer to all Christians of all time. One example is this: *"And hath put all things under his feet, and gave him to be the head over all things to the church, Which is his body, the fulness of him that filleth all in all"* (Eph. 1:22-23). According to the Bible the only sense in which the church universal has organization is that Jesus Christ is the head, and the body is subject to him. This teaching of the word of God is violated by many in a variety of ways. Some have one man who is the earthly head of the church as they view it, some have their conferences, conventions, or other meetings to set policies for the denomination they represent, all of which disregard what God has said about the matter.

Paul taught the same thing in every church concerning the work of the church. The work God has given the church to do involves the preaching of the gospel to the lost. In Paul's first letter to Timothy he said the church is the pillar and ground of the truth (1 Tim. 3:14-15). A part of what that statement is teaching is the church is to cause the truth to be taught, or to engage in the work of preaching it. The word of the Lord was sounded forth from the church at Thessalonica (1 Thess. 1:8). Another way in which the church in the first century was engaged in the work of evangelism was in providing support for those who were preaching the word. Paul received wages from churches to do service to the Corinthians (2 Cor. 11:8).

The Lord made provisions for and gave the church responsibility to edify itself. He gave some apostles who were guided by the Holy Spirit to teach the truth (Eph. 4:11; Acts 2:1-4). He gave some to be prophets who also taught his word as well as, in some cases, predict future events. There were evangelists in the church who heralded the good news of salvation in Christ Jesus. Another group mentioned are pastors and teachers (some say this refers to teaching pastors). Whether this has to do with two groups or different terms referring to the same group the work they are given to do is to teach faithfully what has been revealed by the Holy Spirit. The purpose for which God has given these is to equip the church that it may edify itself (Eph. 4:11-16). What Paul taught the church at Ephesus he taught in every church. Therefore if one church was equipped and required to edify itself then so was every other church. Where, then, does the New Testament authorize the church to do its work of edifying itself through some man-made organization?

From time to time there are those among the saints who have physical and material needs. The Lord provided for their needs to be met. A situation arose in Jerusalem soon after the church began. There were some who had need, and others did what they could to provide for their needs. Some even sold their possessions and goods in order to do so. The number of the disciples was multiplied, and some were being neglected in the daily ministration, and there was a murmuring against some. The matter was brought to the attention of the apostles, and men were selected from among them to solve the problem. They did not form another organization in order to do so, but took care of it themselves (Acts 6:1-6). In addition to the church helping the needy among them there are occasions mentioned in the Bible of churches sending to other churches when they were unable to provide for the needs of their own. There was a dearth in the land of Judea and the brethren in Antioch sent relief to the elders by the hand of Barnabas and Saul (Acts 11:27-30). There are other passages dealing with this same subject, but none of them teaches the church is to take care of any except needy saints. Specific mention is made concerning widows who are widows indeed (1 Tim. 5:3-16). Many of the churches of Christ in the first century did as they were instructed thus showing Paul was effective in his preaching. Let us not fail to do as the Bible teaches on this subject.

This Also Indicates Congregational Independence

The expressions *"in every church"* (1 Cor. 4:17) and *"in all churches"* (1 Cor. 7:17) indicate they were independent. This letter written by the inspired apostle was addressed to *"the church of God at Corinth"* (1 Cor. 1:2) indicates the independent nature of local congregations. Paul wrote that he received wages from churches (2 Cor. 11:8). These churches acted independently according to the plan of God for this work he gave the church to do. Paul did not receive wages from a sponsoring church or a missionary society. No such existed at that time, and none has the scriptural right to exist today. From this we can learn that not only was Paul's preaching effective, but that God's plan of congregational independence is effective also. Bible students have no difficulty recognizing the effectiveness of this plan when we observe a congregation that is led astray by false teacher or teachers and other local congregations remain loyal to the Lord. More Christians become personally involved in the work of reaching the lost with the gospel when God's plan is followed.

There were elders (plural) in every church (singular) (Acts 14:23). This passage alone does not give us all the information God has given on the independent nature of churches of Christ; Peter wrote that these men are to tend the flock of God among them, which teaches that their oversight is limited to the local church where they were appointed (1 Pet. 5:1-3). When this principle is applied it leaves no room for the centralized programs such as are prevalent in many places today. If Paul taught one church to be a sponsoring church then he taught all of them to be a sponsoring church, but this could not be for that would leave none to provide the funds for the sponsoring churches to put on their programs or else they would be sending money back and forth to fund their specific programs, which is in fact what is happening. We ask, therefore, where is the Bible authority for elders of one church to oversee the flock of another local church, a practice that is very common in many local churches of our time?

Paul Taught the Same Thing in Every Church That There May Be Unity of Practice

Preaching the Same Thing in All Churches Destroys the Foundation of Denominationalism. The denominational concept of the church is that the universal church is made up of all the different denominations each continuing to teach and practice their peculiar doctrines. Denominationalism means division, and the preaching of different doctrines is a primary cause of division. Therefore, if all preachers preached the same thing, denominationalism would cease to be.

To further show the inconsistency of denominationalism consider this: Why is it wrong in the eyes of sober thinking men for one man to preach one thing at one place, and something directly opposite that at another place, and yet acceptable for one man to teach one thing at one place and a different man preach something different somewhere else?

The church at Corinth was divided because they were following men, and they were condemned for doing so. Here is what Paul wrote to them about this: *"Now I beseech you, brethren, by the name of our Lord Jesus Christ, that ye all speak the same thing, and that there be no divisions among you; but that ye be perfectly joined together in the same mind and in the same judgment. For it hath been declared unto me of you, my brethren, by them which are of the house of Chloe, that there are contentions among you. Now this I say, that every one of you saith, I am of Paul; and I of Apollos; and I of Cephas; and I of Christ. Is Christ divided? Was Paul crucified for you? Or were ye baptized in the name of Paul?"* (1 Cor. 1:10-13).

Preaching the Same Thing in All Churches Contributes to Unity. No doubt Paul was aware of the prayer Jesus prayed for unity. Here is what he said, *"Neither pray I for these alone, but* *for them also which shall believe on me through their word; That they all may be one; as thou, Father, art in me, and I in thee, that they also may be one in us: that the world may believe that thou hast sent me. And the glory which thou gavest me I have given them; that they may be one, even as we are one"* (John 17:20-22). Jesus not only prayed that his apostles might be one, but that all who believe in him through their word might be one. The oneness Jesus prayed for was the same as that which exists with Jesus and the Father. A result of the kind of unity Jesus prayed for is that the world might believe that God sent him. For this unity to be a reality all the apostles would have had to preach the same thing, and that is what happened as we can see by reading in the Bible what they preached. Can we not see from this that a contributing factor to the division that exists in the religious world is the division among those who profess to be disciples of Christ?

Paul also knew the basis of the unity Jesus prayed for is the word of God. Unity that is based upon anything more than or less than the word of God cannot be the unity Jesus prayed for. There is a possibility that some can have unity based upon the doctrines and commandments of men, but that is not the unity the Bible speaks about. Those who preach any doctrine that differs from what the apostles preached are causing division among professed believers, not the unity we are considering in this study. In his first letter to the church at Corinth Paul told them, *"Now I beseech you, brethren, by the name of our Lord Jesus Christ, that ye all speak the same thing, and that there be no divisions among you; but that ye be perfectly joined together in the same mind and in the same judgment"* (1 Cor. 1:10). This statement was written to a church that exalted some men, and was divided. The same is true in many places today, and therefore the teaching is needed now as much as ever. Note that this letter was written to all that in every place call upon the Lord Jesus Christ (1 Cor. 1:2).

This same apostle wrote to the saints at Ephesus, *"I therefore, the prisoner of the Lord, beseech you that ye walk worthy of the vocation wherewith ye are called, with all lowliness and meekness, with longsuffering, forbearing one another in love; endeavoring to keep the unity of the Spirit in the bond of peace"* (Eph. 4:1-3). The unity he beseeches them to keep is the unity of the Spirit.

This would be the unity that is based on the teaching of the Holy Spirit. Since the Holy Spirit guided men to write the Scriptures we have today, and is not now guiding men except through the revealed word of God this would refer to unity that is based on what the Bible teaches. That it is to be done in the bond of peace teaches that the manner in which we go about to maintain the unity is not that of those who make their own rules and write their own creed books. Neither is it accomplished by those who refuse to consider all the Bible says on a given subject and are unwilling to consider the possibility they might be wrong because they have only studied a part of it. The unity of the Spirit is not attained or maintained by misrepresenting those with whom one may differ and refusing to hear what he has to say on the matter

When we differ with someone on what we perceive to be a doctrinal matter are we more interested in winning a point with him than we are in coming to an agreement on what the Bible teaches? Are we interested enough in maintaining unity among brethren that we will give up our opinions, and contend for the faith only when we are certain that it is the faith we are contending for, and not our personal ideas or programs? We should be more concerned about why we differ, and try to agree on what the Bible teaches than in having our own way when differences arise.

The unity of the Spirit says there is one body, and one Spirit, one hope, one Lord, one faith, one baptism, and one God (Eph. 4:4-6). Accepting the fact there is one God and one Lord Jesus Christ while teaching there are many bodies, many faiths, and several baptisms is not the way to have the unity of the Spirit. The Scriptures teach the body is the church (Eph. 1:22- 23; Col. 1:24), yet many thank God for the many churches and they can join the church of their choice.

Some say there is the baptism of the Holy Spirit that some are experiencing now, and that if one desires to be baptized in water he has the choice of sprinkling, pouring, or a burial, but the Bible says there is one baptism. There was a time when some received the baptism of the Holy Spirit, but that was before Paul wrote to the Ephesians saying, *"there is one baptism."* Can we not see we are guilty of rejecting the authority of God's word when we accept there is one God but say there are many bodies, faiths, and baptisms?

Chapter Five

Admonishing and Teaching Every Man

(Colossians 1:24-29)

Do you want to preach like Paul? Do you want to listen to those who preach like Paul? Any one who desires to preach or lend his support to preachers would do well to learn what he can from studying the life of Paul, giving special attention to why he preached as he did. Even a casual reading shows that it was a desire to save souls that motivated Paul to preach the gospel as he did. But there is more for us to learn about why he was such an effective preacher of the gospel of Jesus Christ. There are some specific statements in the Scriptures by and about him that indicate that he preached what he did the way he did to more effectively accomplish this purpose. Paul was always ready to put forth a great effort to do this, and willing at any time to suffer for Christ, and rejoice in doing so. The gospel of Christ is the only thing that will save the souls of men, and Paul knew this very well. He was made a minister to fulfill the word of God and that included the mystery that had been hid from ages and from generations, but at that time was made manifest to all his saints. This is a good place to point out that there are mysteries that we will never know, but there are some mysteries we can know because God has revealed them. God knew what the mystery was, but man did not know because we can know what is in the mind of God only as he reveals it to us. The Bible says, *"For what man knoweth the things of a man, save the spirit of man which is in him? Even so the things of God knoweth no man, but the Spirit of God"* (1 Cor. 2:11). We learn from other statements in the New Testament that the first century disciples preached Christ. Soon after the gospel was preached the first time in Jerusalem Philip went down to Samaria and preached Christ unto them (Acts 8:5). He also preached Christ to the eunuch from Ethiopia (Acts 8:35).

Paul said he preached Christ to the people of Colossae saying, *"Whom we preach, warning every man, and teaching every man in all wisdom"* (Col. 1:28). This method is one that is used in view of things that are wrong and call for a warning. A person who experiences severe chest pains will usually recognize that as a warning he is about to have a heart attack. Any time one is engaged in wrongdoing he needs to be warned or admonished. The apostle said he warned *"every man."* He knew that every man is valuable to the Lord, and wanted to leave no one out. This word is also used to show us the purpose of the written word of God. The Israelites were engaged in wrong during their wilderness wanderings, and Paul wrote the Corinthians to admonish them not to follow their example, *"Now all these things happened unto them for examples: and they are written for our admonition, upon whom the ends of the world are come"* (1 Cor. 10:11).

The same word is used to show fathers how they are to bring up their children that they may become the kind of people that will please the Lord. He wrote, *"And, ye fathers, provoke not your children to wrath: but bring them up in the nurture and admonition of the Lord"* (Eph. 6:4). Children do things that are wrong at times, and need to be warned not to do them. Parents are charged with the responsibility of giving that warning to them. Heretics are to be admonished (shown wherein they are wrong) before being rejected (Tit. 3:10). Heretics are those who promote factions or divisions among the people of God, and we need to be warned against such actions. These people need to be warned first for they are to be rejected if they do not heed the warning. Every person who would seek to please God and enter heaven in the end needs to receive this kind of warning. Any one who reads the writings of the apostle Paul cannot help but be impressed with the fact this was characteristic of the preaching he did. An example of this is the statement he made to the elders of the church of Ephesus. He said to them, *"Therefore watch, and remember, that by the space of three years I ceased not to warn every one night and day with tears"* (Acts 20:31). One of the responsibilities of elders who have the oversight of the flock of God among them is to admonish them (1 Thess. 5:12). Brethren who are unfaithful are to be admonished (2 Thess. 3:15).

Admonishing was a vital part of the preaching done by one of the most effective preachers of all time, the apostle Paul, and so also was teaching. Teaching differs from admonishing in that it has to do chiefly with the impartation of positive truth. Knowledge of God and his word is essential to being the kind of person God approves of. Teaching has always had a prominent role in man's relationship with God. God taught Adam and Eve what he expected of them when he created them and placed them in the Garden of Eden. He also taught Noah, Abraham, Jacob and others who lived in that period of time. During the time the Law of Moses was in effect the fathers of the households were told to teach their children diligently (Deut. 6:6-9). To be a citizen in the kingdom of Christ one must first of all be taught. Jeremiah prophesied that under the covenant God would make, when the Law of Moses was taken out of the way and nailed to the cross of Christ, all under the covenant would be taught of God (Jer. 31:31-34). The writer of the book of Hebrews tells us this prophecy was fulfilled, and that all shall know the Lord (Heb. 8:6-13). Jesus said that one must be taught of God in order to come to him. *"No man can come to me, except the Father which hath sent me draw him: and I will raise him up at the last day. It is written in the prophets, And they shall be all taught of God. Every man therefore that hath heard, and hath learned of the Father, cometh unto me"* (John 6:44-45).

Preaching that is devoid of teaching is most ineffective in bringing lost souls to a knowledge of the truth that makes men free from sin when they believe and obey it. Jesus said, *"Ye shall know the truth, and the truth shall make you free"* (John 8:32), and Peter wrote, *"Seeing ye have purified your souls in obeying the truth through the Spirit unto unfeigned love of the brethren, see that ye love one another with a pure heart fervently"* (1 Pet. 1:22). Before the New Testament was written the Lord sent out preachers who were guided by the Holy Spirit to teach all things he taught them. In this way the hearers received the evidence that enabled them to believe and thereby call upon the name of the Lord that they might be saved. They could not believe unless they heard, and they could not hear without a preacher (see Rom. 10:13-17). The Lord sent the preachers, and they spoke as the Spirit gave them utterance (Acts 2:1-4). Many of the people who heard them preach believed in the Lord Jesus Christ. We can have the same faith they had by reading the account of their preaching that is recorded in the New Testament. Though we do not have the miraculous guidance of the Holy Spirit today, we can be effective in preaching if we admonish and teach as we let the word of Christ dwell in us richly (Col. 3:16).

The passage under study just here says that Paul preached Christ, warning every man and teaching every man in all wisdom. In a previous chapter we noted that Paul said he preached to the Corinthians as he did that their faith should not stand in the wisdom of man, but in the power of God (1 Cor. 2:5). He then reminded them that they spoke the wisdom of God (v. 7). Peter attested to the fact that Paul wrote according to the wisdom given unto him. This tells us that Paul did not write his own ideas or what he had been taught by man, but what was revealed to him by the Holy Spirit of God. Some of what Paul wrote was hard to understand, and those who were unlearned and unstable wrested or perverted it, as they did other Scriptures. They did this to their own destruction (2 Pet. 3:15-16). Wresting or perverting the Scriptures did not end with those who lived in the first century. There are still some who are guilty of the same today.

It is a perversion of the Scriptures to teach that men can be saved by faith only for the Bible plainly says that we are justified by works, and not by faith only (Jas. 2:24). To teach one is saved by faith only also denies some plain statements in the word of God such as, *"He that believeth and is baptized shall be saved"* (Mark 16:16*), "Arise and be baptized, and wash away thy sins"* *(*Acts 22:16) and *"The like figure whereunto baptism doth also now save us"* (1 Pet. 3:21).

Those who teach that Christians are authorized to use mechanical instruments of music in their worship to God must pervert the Scriptures in their attempt. If they believe, as many of them do, that we must have scriptural authority for what we do in our worship, then it is their responsibility to show Bible authority for their practice. It is true that such instruments were used during the time the law of Moses was in effect, but that law was taken out of the way and nailed to the cross of Jesus Christ (Col. 2:14), and a new law put into effect (Heb. 8:6-13; 10:9). The teaching of the covenant of Christ on this subject is for Christians to sing (1 Cor. 14:15; Eph. 5:19; Col. 3:16). There is no authority in the New Testament for Christians to use mechanical instruments of music in their worship to God.

Men of today have many false concepts concerning the church that Jesus bought with his blood. The Scriptures teach it is a spiritual kingdom with a spiritual mission. Yet many try to make it a social institution designed to cure all the social ills of the world. The wisdom by which Paul wrote says, *"For the kingdom of God is not meat and drink; but righteousness, and peace, and joy in the Holy Spirit"* (Rom. 14:18). It is therefore a perversion of Scripture for the church to use the money contributed by its members to build and maintain institutions whose primary function is to entertain and otherwise provide for the social needs of the people.

Why Did Paul Admonish And Teach Every Man In All Wisdom?

We let Paul answer this question for us. He said it was *"that we may present every man perfect in Christ Jesus"* (Col. 1:28). The word "perfect" is used in the Bible to refer to those who are mature or full grown children of God. The teaching of Jesus in the Sermon on the Mount was to the end that we may be perfect or mature (Matt. 5:48). This is a state all are admonished to strive for. Paul did not consider that he was already perfect, but pressed forward that he might do so (Phil. 3:12-15). It is a state that is attainable for all who will give heed to the sound teaching of the word of God such as Paul and other inspired men of the first century did. Some then had failed to do so, but needed someone to teach them the first principles of the oracles or God. They were told to go on unto perfection (Heb. 5:12-6:1a).

This great apostle was well aware of the need for every child of God to be edified, and did much preaching to that end. He wrote that cleansing ourselves of all filthiness of the flesh and spirit is necessary to perfect holiness in the fear of God (2 Cor. 7:1). Epaphras, a servant of Christ from Colossae, labored fervently for them in prayers, to the end that they might stand perfect and complete in all the will of God (Col. 4:12). Paul wanted to see the Thessalonians' face that he might perfect what was lacking in their faith (1 Thess. 3:10). Not only in his preaching, but also in his personal conduct he was careful to do only what would edify others. He wrote to the church of God at Corinth that all things were lawful for him, but all things did not edify. Therefore he sought to please others rather than himself, not seeking his own profit, but the profit of many, that their soul may be saved (1 Cor. 10:23, 33). He also instructed them that all they did should be unto edifying (1 Cor. 14:26). In his second letter to the same people he reminded them that he did all things for their edifying. He expressed deep concern for them by referring to them as *"dearly beloved."*

The relationship in which one can reach this state of completeness is in Christ. The Bible teaches that we are complete in him (Col. 2:10). In order to be complete one must enter that relationship by being baptized into Christ. Two statements in the New Testament tell us that we are baptized into Christ. They are: *"Know ye not, that so many of us as were baptized into Jesus Christ were baptized into his death?"* (Rom. 6:3), and *"For as many of you as have been baptized into Christ have put on Christ"* (Gal. 3:27). This is the only way, according to the word of God, that one can get into Christ and enjoy this completeness found there. Not only did Paul preach orally, warning every man, and teaching every man in all wisdom, that he may present every man perfect in Christ, but wrote as he was guided by the Holy Spirit knowing that the Scriptures inspired of God are able to make the man of God perfect, furnishing him completely unto every good work (2 Tim. 3:16-17).

It is a noble and worthy effort to admonish and teach every man to the end that we may present every man perfect in Christ Jesus, but this can only be accomplished by those who are willing to receive and act upon such preaching. May the Lord give us more men who will strive to be more effective in preaching Christ, and more people who will receive and obey the gospel of Jesus Christ.

Chapter Six

He Shunned Not to Declare All the Counsel of God

(Acts 20:17-27)

Paul rarely spent more than a few weeks in a city preaching the gospel of Jesus Christ before going on to some other place. Ephesus was one exception to that. The information we have concerning the work he did there indicates a great deal of interest in that church. He not only spent time in the city preaching, he wrote a letter to the saints there and also met with the elders of that church on the island of Miletus. He reminded them of the way he conducted himself and taught them while he was in their midst preaching the gospel. Among the things he said to them was that he had kept back nothing that was profitable for them, and had taught them publicly and from house to house (Acts 20:20). Their profit in spiritual matters was Paul's concern, and he did his part in seeing that they had every opportunity to enjoy all the spiritual blessings that are in Christ (Eph. 1:3). Any one who preaches would do well to learn what this means, why Paul thought this was so important, and then make an earnest effort to follow his example.

Paul Declared All the Counsel of God

Everything Paul taught them was profitable for them, and nothing was left out that would profit them in spiritual matters. One cannot help but be reminded of a statement Paul wrote to Timothy later in which he pointed out that all Scripture is inspired of God and is profitable, and will make the man of God perfect thoroughly furnishing him unto every good work (2 Tim. 3:16-17). Serving the Lord in all humility of mind as Paul did makes the message of the gospel more effective. How many of us would continue to declare all the counsel of God if we experienced the same tears and temptations he did because he boldly taught God's word as it was revealed to him? Many who are preaching today seem to show more interest in personal popularity than in preaching that which saves the souls of those who will believe it. If a thing is profitable to the hearers the preacher should not avoid it just because it might not be the most popular thing to do. Declaring all the counsel of God demands that we condemn all sin, and tell the hearers all that he requires for salvation, and neither add anything to that or leave any of it out.

He Preached Publicly and From House to House

There will always be a need for the public preaching of the gospel. Because of many changes being made in technology the ways of getting the message from the speaker to the people may vary. Some of these techniques are more effective than others, often depending on the culture, the facilities, the speaker, and the audience. One thing to remember is that, regardless of the techniques, equipment, size of audience, etc., it is the gospel of Christ that must be preached in order to be effective in winning souls to Christ. Modern techniques can be helpful in getting the lessons across to the hearers, but they can also be a hindrance. Seeing that which illustrates or amplifies what the teacher desires to impart to the students is helpful, but that which detracts from that message gets in the way of the learning process. Preachers can become so dependent on helps they have a difficult time teaching a lesson when there are no such helps available.

Some of the most effective teaching of the word of God has been done in a private way. Jesus taught the woman he met at the well in Samaria the valuable lesson on the subject of worship. She was convinced he was the Christ, and went to tell others she had found the man who told her all things she had ever done. She then asked, *"Is this not the Christ?"* (John 4:29). He was speaking to one man about the necessity of being born again of water and of the Spirit in order to enter the kingdom of heaven (John 3:1-8). Philip, the evangelist, left a large group of people and went down a road where he came in contact with one man, a eunuch from Ethiopia, and preached Christ unto him (Acts 8:35-38). There are men today in various parts of the world who spend their time making contacts and teaching individuals the gospel of the Lord, and some of them with a great deal of success.

Paul did not have access to power point, overhead projectors, charts (cloth, paper, or otherwise), chalk boards, etc., yet he was effective in reaching the lost with the truth that saves men's souls. Whether he was in a prison, a synagogue, or traveling along the way, when he had an opportunity he preached God's word.

Paul preached publicly and from house to house, declaring all the counsel of God. The counsel of God refers to all the contents of his divine plan to save men's souls. The Bible tells us of some who rejected the counsel of God. John the Baptist learned of the work and miracles of Jesus in the region around Capernaum and Nain, and sent two of his disciples to ask Jesus whether he was the one to come or whether they should look for another. Jesus instructed them to go tell John of the miracles he did, and then spoke to the people concerning John. Some were baptized with the baptism of John, but others *"rejected the counsel of God against themselves, being not baptized of him"* (Luke 7:29-30). From this we can understand why it is so important to declare *all* the counsel of God in our preaching. Another reason to declare all the counsel of God is the fact that his counsel is immutable. The writer of the book of Hebrews declared, *"Wherein God, willing more abundantly to show unto the heirs of promise the immutability of his counsel, confirmed it by an oath: That by two immutable things, in which it was impossible for God to lie, we might have a strong consolation, who have fled for refuge to lay hold upon the hope before us"* (Heb. 6:17-18).

The psalmist declared, *"The sum of thy word is truth; And every one of thy righteous ordinances endureth for ever"* (Ps. 119:160, ASV). In the light of such a plain statement how can any one expect to please God and leave out some of what he has said in his word? Yet there are many prominent and popular preachers who promise salvation on much less than what is found in the word of God. One of the most popular doctrines being taught today is that salvation is by faith only, or all that one has to do in order to be saved is to accept Jesus as his personal Savior. This doctrine is not found in the word of God, but rather is shown to be false. Accepting the sum of what the gospel teaches one to do to be saved we learn that one must hear the word for the word of God is the source of saving faith (Rom. 10:17). The Lord also requires that we repent of our sins, a command given to all men (Acts 17:30-31). Jesus said if we confess him before men he will confess us before the Father (Matt. 10:32-33). Jesus promised salvation to those who believe and are baptized (Mark 16:16), and his apostles told their hearers they would receive remission of sins if they repented and were baptized (Acts 2:38). It is generally known that many preachers are saying to their hearers that some of these things are not necessary. Are they effective in winning souls to Christ or in reality are they deceiving them into thinking they are saved while failing to obey some of the commandments of the Lord?

Fear of trials, persecutions, imprisonments or other unjust treatment did not prevent Paul from preaching what those in his audience needed. He preached righteousness, self-control, and the judgment to come to Felix because that was what he needed to hear (Acts 24:25). He condemned idolatry and preached the one true God in Athens and in Ephesus because they were cities given over to idolatry (Acts 17, 18, 19). These are but two of the many examples that could be cited to show what Paul thought about the need for declaring all the counsel of God. All the counsel of God for us today is found in the New Testament, and the only way we can preach all the counsel of God is to preach all the New Testament says.

This reminds me that one of the best ways for preachers today to declare all the counsel of God is to do more expository preaching. In this type of sermons you select a verse, paragraph, chapter, or book of the Bible and analyze or explain its contents. Admittedly this is one of the most difficult types of sermons to prepare and present effectively, but it is also one of the best ways to teach what the Bible says. This is a good way for preachers to increase their knowledge of the Scriptures, and help others understand the teaching of the Bible more clearly and completely.

Paul Taught on the Subject of Stewardship
Paul realized he had been entrusted with the gospel, and ac-

cepted the responsibility willingly. He wrote to the Corinthians, "For though I preach the gospel, I have nothing to glory of: for necessity is laid upon me; yea, woe is unto me, if I preach not the gospel! For if I do this thing willingly, I have a reward: but if against my will, a dispensation (stewardship, NKJV) of the gospel is committed unto me. What is my reward then? Verily that, when I preach the gospel, I may make the gospel of Christ without charge, that I abuse not my power in the gospel. For though I be free from all men, yet have I made myself servant unto all, that I might gain the more." (1 Cor. 9:16-19). He used the same word in writing to the Ephesians and Colossians, telling them that the dispensation (stewardship) of the grace of God had been given to him for their benefit. This revelation that was given to him was a mystery which in other ages was not made known, but was revealed to him by the Holy Spirit of God. Once it had been revealed it was no longer a mystery, and by reading what he wrote they could have the same understanding of that mystery that Paul had (Eph. 3:1-5). Included in the mystery was that the Gentiles should be "fellow heirs, and of the same body, and partakers of his promise in Christ by the gospel" (Eph. 3:6). The same thought is presented in Colossians 1:25-29. The dispensation of the grace of God was given to Paul by revelation, as it was to all the apostles, and with it came the responsibility to faithfully proclaim it. By doing so Paul was an effective preacher. We have the same message in the inspired word of God, and also have the responsibility of handling it aright. To fail to do so, either by perverting it, wresting it, adding to it, or taking away from it, will bring the rejection of God upon us (Gal. 1:6-9; 2 Pet. 3:16; Rev. 22:18-19).

What is stewardship? Stewardship is the management of that which belongs to another, but has been entrusted to us to use, and for which we must give account. It is the administration of the property of another. There is a sense in which everything we are and everything we have was given to us by God to use, and for which we must give account to him at a time he chooses. This is included in this statement of Paul "For we must all appear before the judgment seat of Christ; that every one may receive the things done in his body, according to that he hath done, whether it be good or bad." (2 Cor. 5:10).

God has entrusted us with all that we have, and that makes us stewards. He made man out of the dust of the ground and breathed in his nostrils the breath of life, giving him physical life. He put him in the garden of Eden where he had access to the tree of life (Gen. 2:7-9). Eating of the fruit of the tree of life would enable him to live forever. Paul told the people of Athens that God gives to all life, breath, and all things (Acts 17:25). In the light of such plain irrefutable language how can any one show such disrespect for human life as many are doing?

What Paul and other writers of the New Testament said about the way we are to use our time teaches us that we are stewards of time. Paul wrote to the Ephesians and the Colossians that they should redeem the time (Eph. 5:15-16; Col. 4:5). To redeem is to buy it up or make proper use of it. Preachers who declare all the counsel of God tell their hearers they should not waste their time, but use it to the glory of God. What are you doing with that which God has entrusted to you?

Our bodies God has given us are not really ours, but belong to him who made us. Paul wrote, "What? know ye not that your body is the temple of the Holy Ghost which is in you, which ye have of God, and ye are not your own? For ye are bought with a price: therefore glorify God in your body, and in your spirit, which are God's" (1 Cor. 6:19-20). Paul also gave some instructions as to how we are to use our bodies. "I beseech you therefore, brethren, by the mercies of God, that ye present your bodies a living sacrifice, holy, acceptable unto God, which is your reasonable service. And be not conformed to this world: but be ye transformed by the renewing of your mind, that ye may prove what is that good, and acceptable, and perfect, will of God" (Rom. 12:1-2). The proper use of our bodies would include using our tongues to teach others the truth and praise his name, and our hands to minister to the needs of others. Of course other members of our bodies have their proper use also.

All of us have some talents God has given to us. Some have more than others, each according to his ability to use them. Jesus taught this lesson in the parable of the talents (Matt. 25:14-30). A vital lesson taught in this parable is that acceptance or rejection of the Lord is determined by whether we use the talent(s) that have been given to us. The servants in this parable who received five and two talents respectively were not rewarded because of the number of talents they received, neither was the one talent man condemned because he had only one talent. What the Lord requires of stewards is for them to be faithful as Paul wrote to the Corinthians (1 Cor. 4:1-2).

Whatever amount of wealth one may have control of it is not really his, but belongs to the Lord. It is God who gives us the power to get wealth (Deut. 8:18). The attitude we are to have toward riches indicates there is a right way and a wrong way to use them. Paul told Timothy to charge them that are minded to be rich not to be high minded, nor trust in uncertain riches, but to trust in the living God for it is God who gives us richly all things to enjoy (1 Tim. 6:17). He continues by saying that when we use our wealth as God intends we will lay up for ourselves a good foundation for the time to come, no doubt referring to the time of reckoning when the Lord will repay for faithful service (1 Tim. 6:18-19). For preachers of today to be effective in winning souls they need to use their own money properly, and teach others to do the same.

Jesus also taught on the subject of stewardship. What Paul taught agrees with what Jesus taught. At least twenty-nine of the parables Jesus told (about 83% of all of them) deal with some aspect of stewardship. This shows not only the vastness of the subject, but also the importance the Lord gave to it.

This Stewardship Includes All Christians
Let us consider first the stewardship of elders or bishops. On this subject Paul wrote, "For a bishop must be blameless, as the steward of God; not selfwilled, not soon angry, not given to wine, no striker, not given to filthy lucre" (Tit. 1:7). There is a great need in the church of the Lord today for qualified men to oversee the flock of God among them. Members of the church are commanded to, "Obey them that have the rule over you, and submit yourselves: for they watch for your souls, as they that must give account, that they may do it with joy, and not with grief: for that is unprofitable for you" (Heb. 13:17). This Scripture says that elders are to give account indicating a stewardship is involved. A failure on their part

to do so often results in weak members wandering away from the fold and never returning. Effective preachers recognize the need is present in every generation and will teach what is needed to develop men for this great work. The qualifications for those who would be faithful stewards in watching in behalf of souls are such that men need to begin early in life developing them, and thereby are ready when they are old enough and experienced enough to faithfully shepherd the flock of God.

Effective teachers will show from the Scriptures that men who desire the office of a bishop must take heed to themselves (Acts 20:28). The seriousness of the duties of such work demands that a rigid self-examination be done. This should include such things as making sure they possess the qualities of leadership that will enable them to cause others to want to follow their example. Essential to the development of these qualifications is knowledge of the word of God to which he must hold fast that he may be able to both exhort and convict the gainsayers (Tit. 1:9).

They are also instructed to take heed to the flock. They need to know the flock as shepherds know their sheep. They need to know something about who they are, where they live, how they live, and what their needs, both physical and spiritual, may be. Peter wrote that elders are to feed the flock of God among them (1 Pet. 5:2). This would involve providing them with the spiritual diet they need: milk for the babes (1 Pet. 2:1-2), and meat for the more mature (Heb. 5:12-14). In taking heed to the flock they are to guard against those who would teach perverse things and draw away disciples to themselves (Acts 20:28-31). A failure on the part of some elders to expose false teachers and false teaching continues to cause confusion and division among the Lord's people. Paul did not hesitate to warn everyone night and day with tears about such matters, and neither will effective preachers of today. Elders who take their work seriously recognize the damage there can be to a congregation when sin is allowed to go unnoticed and unchallenged. Therefore they will take the lead in exercising disciplinary action when it is needed to maintain the purity of the church. The church at Thessalonica was taught to withdraw from every brother who walked disorderly, and not according to the tradition they received from the apostles (2 Thess. 3:6). One purpose for this action is to make the guilty party ashamed to the end they may be saved (2 Thess. 3:14; 1 Cor. 5:5).

There is a reward promised those who fulfill their responsibility as faithful stewards. Paul told Timothy that those who rule well should be counted worthy of double honor (1 Tim. 5:17). Peter said that when the chief Shepherd comes they would receive a crown of glory that does not fade away (1 Pet. 5:4).

Preachers have received a stewardship. Paul was speaking of himself and other apostles when he wrote that they were stewards of the mysteries of Christ (1 Cor. 4:1), and to the Ephesians when he wrote that he had received the dispensation (stewardship) of the grace of God (Eph. 3:2). However, who would doubt that a stewardship was involved that includes all Christians when he told Timothy to commit to faithful men what he had received from him (2 Tim. 2:2), and the charge to him to preach the word (2 Tim. 4:2). Every man who decides to prepare himself to preach the unsearchable riches of Christ must recognize he has something entrusted to him which he is to use for its intended purpose, and for which he will be required to give account some day. Preachers acting as faithful and wise stewards would eliminate much of the efforts among gospel preachers to destroy the influence, defame the character, impugn the motives, misrepresent the purpose, improperly classify, bring in line by pressure those with whom they differ on some points. To discharge this responsibility faithfully he must take heed to himself and to the doctrine (1 Tim. 4:16). In doing so he will save both himself and those who hear him. What a great reward, even in this life. A crown of righteousness is promised those who love the appearing of the Lord (2 Tim. 4:8).

Effective preachers remind parents they have a stewardship. Children are gifts from God to parents who have the responsibility of training them in the way they should go. In his letter to the saints at Ephesus Paul wrote, "And, ye fathers, provoke not your children to wrath: but bring them up in the nurture and admonition of the Lord" (Eph. 6:4). Bringing up children involves instruction in such things as the fear of the Lord that the Bible says is both the beginning of knowledge and wisdom (Prov. 1:7; Ps. 111: 10). They need to know this because to fear God and keep his commandments is the whole duty of man (Eccl. 12:13). In view of the many efforts being made today to remove God from the thinking of mankind it will take great effort on the part of all Christians to give our children the teaching they need to counteract these false claims. Timothy's mother and grandmother knew the value of beginning early to teach him the word of God (2 Tim. 1:5). He was also reminded in this same letter that the word of God, which he had known from a child, was able to make him wise unto salvation (2 Tim. 3:15). In addition to instruction corrective discipline is necessary at times to achieve the desired end. Children become unruly at times, some more than others, and must be corrected. Eli's children made themselves vile, and he restrained them not (1 Sam. 3:13). The end result was that his house was not purged with sacrifice nor offering forever (v. 14). The wise man said that a child left to himself will bring his mother to shame (Prov. 29:15). A good way to guard against this is to chasten them as the need arises remembering that "no chastening for the present seemeth to be joyous, but grievous: nevertheless afterward it yieldeth the peaceable fruit of righteousness unto them which are exercised thereby" (Heb. 12:11). As preachers of the gospel of Jesus Christ let us do all we can to help parents train their children to be useful servants in the kingdom of God.

What Kind of Stewards Does God Want?

Peter wrote, "As every man hath received the gift, even so minister the same one to another, as good stewards of the manifold grace of God" (1 Pet. 4:10). Worthy of note in this passage is the fact every man has received something from God, and is expected to make use of it as a good steward. The application Peter makes of this is found in the next verse. The rule is applied first to speaking. He said, "If any man speak, let him speak as the oracles of God." The oracles of God have to do with the words God has uttered. Stephen referred to that which Moses received at Mt. Sinai as "living oracles" (Acts 7:38). Paul said the Jews had advantage over the Gentiles "because unto them were committed the oracles of God" (Rom. 3:2). Therefore when we speak as the oracles of God we are saying exactly what God has revealed, nothing more and nothing less. Good stewards will also minister as God has supplied us with the ability to do so. God has given us some natural abilities and expects us to use them to help others who are in need (Rom. 12:4-8). This Scripture teaches us that the end result of this is that God will be glorified. Good stewards want to do what will bring glory and honor to their master. This should be our desire.

God wants faithful and wise stewards. Paul told the Corinthians that it is required in stewards that a man be found faithful (1 Cor. 4:1-2). Faithful stewards ascertain the nature of the duty that is imposed upon them. They will also faithfully perform that duty, doing what they do heartily as unto the Lord, and not unto men (Col. 2:23). Jesus talked about a faithful and wise steward, and said such would be rewarded (Luke 12:42-44).

With stewardship there comes a reckoning. We are account-able for the use we make of what has been entrusted to us. Jesus told a parable of an unjust steward who was told by his master to give account of his stewardship (Luke 16:1-4). Though he was wise in some ways he was not faithful to his master and was told he could not be a steward any longer. God wants us to be wise in the use we make of what he has given into our care, but wisdom is not enough, he requires faithfulness. We, too, are accountable to God for the use we make of what we have. "For we must all appear before the judgment seat of Christ; that every one may receive the things done in his body, according to that he hath done, whether it be good or bad" (2 Cor. 5:10). Paul makes it clear that this is individual accountability, "But why dost thou judge thy brother? or why dost thou set at nought thy brother? for we shall all stand before the judgment seat of Christ. For it is written, As I live, saith the Lord, every knee shall bow to me, and every tongue shall confess to God. So then every one of us shall give account of himself to God" (Rom. 14:10-12). The reward for the faithful steward includes increased trust. Jesus made this point in the parable of the talents. He said to the five-talent man and to the two-talent man that because they were faithful over a few things he would make them ruler over many things (Matt. 25:21, 23). The man who had the one talent had it taken away from him, and he was cast into outer darkness (Matt. 25:28, 30).

Effective preachers will remind their hearers that we have a stewardship that we have received from God, and that we must give account to him for the use we make of all he has committed to our trust. The promise of a reward can be a great motivation to make the proper use of all God has entrusted to our care. The Lord is coming at a time unknown to us. Therefore let us not be like the servant who said in his heart that his lord delayed his coming and he could do as he pleased lest we be cut asunder as he was (Luke 12:45-46). Rather let us be faithful and wise stewards that we may be blessed of the Lord (Luke 12:42-43).

Paul Taught on the Subject of Marriage

Paul was not a married man, but confirmed his right to "lead about a . . .wife" (1 Cor. 9:5). Contrary to the belief of some he did not teach it was wrong for those to marry who had the right to do so. What he taught on the subject of marriage was in complete harmony with what Jesus taught on the subject. He taught that a woman is bound by the law to her husband as long as he lives, and if she maries another man while her husband is living she shall be called an adulteress. But if her husband is dead she is not an adulteress though she marries another man (Rom. 7:1-3). One of the times Jesus taught on this subject he said, "And I say unto you, Whosoever shall put away his wife, except it be for fornication, and shall marry another, committeth adultery: and whoso marrieth her which is put away doth commit adultery" (Matt. 19:9).

It is not my purpose in this book to explore all the ways the teaching of Paul and of Jesus have been and are being violated, but to call attention to the fact that Jesus gave only one reason for one to put away his/her spouse and marry another without being guilty of adultery, and that is for the cause of fornication. How can we say one is effective in the sight of God if he fails to teach and apply what the New Testament says on this subject? Volumes have been written on this subject: some supporting what Jesus said, and some trying to explain it away. The Bible has much more to say about this subject, but I will let this suffice for the purpose of this book. My intention is that to be best of my ability to be as David said he was, "Therefore I esteem all thy precepts concerning all things to be right; and I hate every false way" (Ps. 119:128).

Some Things Paul Taught Concerning
The Second Coming of Christ

Effective preachers realize the importance of reminding their hearers that Jesus is coming again, and will reward the righteous with everlasting life. They need to know also that those who know not God and obey not the gospel will be punished with everlasting destruction. Paul did that. He lived in hope of eternal life (Tit. 1:2), and fully expected to receive it in due time (2 Tim. 4:8). He said eternal life is promised "To them who by patient continuance in well doing seek for glory and honor and immortality, eternal life" (Rom. 2:7). To the Thessalonians he wrote, "And to you who are troubled rest with us, when the Lord Jesus shall be revealed from heaven with his mighty angels, In flaming fire taking vengeance on them that know not God, and that obey not the gospel of our Lord Jesus Christ: Who shall be punished with everlasting destruction from the presence of the Lord, and from the glory of his power" (2 Thess. 1:7-9).

It should be obvious to the reader that it would be impossible to mention everything included in the oracles of God in such a short book. However, we deem it important to present some things Paul taught on the subject of the second coming of Christ that indicate the effectiveness of his preaching. Some of what he taught on this subject is found in his first letter to the church at Thessalonica. It appears from some of the things he said there was some misunderstanding among them about whether or not those who died before the Lord comes would be saved. He did not want them to be ignorant on this matter. This is what he said, "But I would not have you to be ignorant, brethren, concerning them which are asleep, that ye sorrow not, even as others which have no hope" (1 Thess. 4:13). There are those who have reason to sorrow when some of their loved ones pass away. This is true of those who die in their sins. Jesus said if we die in our sins where he is we cannot go (John 8:21). On the other hand those who die in the Lord are blessed for they shall rest from their labors (Rev. 14:13). The Christians at Thessalonica did have hope: those who had died in the Lord and those who were still living. He wanted them to understand that when the Lord comes all of them would meet the Lord in the clouds, and ever be with the Lord. He concluded this by telling them to comfort one another with these words (1 Thess. 4:14-18). It should be pointed out here that in this passage the apostle is not discussing what will happen to those who die in their sins, only those who have obeyed the Lord and are ready for his coming. Thus when he said, "the dead in Christ shall rise first" (v. 16), he is saying the dead in Christ will rise before those Christians who are still living when Christ comes will be changed. Then both the living and the dead will be caught up together to meet the Lord in the air, and ever be with the Lord. To learn more about what change will take place with the living we go to another letter Paul wrote. This is what he said to the Corinthians, "Behold, I shew you a mystery; We shall not all sleep, but we shall all be changed, In a moment, in the twinkling of an eye, at the last trump: for the trumpet shall sound, and the dead shall be raised incorruptible, and we shall be changed" (1 Cor. 15:51-52). Paul also said that when Jesus comes he will change our vile body that it may be like his glorious body (Phil. 3:20-21).

Paul said that the coming of Jesus will be as a thief in the night (1 Thess. 5:2). Jesus said that only the Father knew of that day and hour, and that in view of the certainty of its coming we should watch and pray (Mark 13:32-33). The most effective preachers of any age are those who have been able to convince sinners that eternal doom awaits all who die in their sins, but that Jesus came to redeem us. We learn from the pen of the apostle Paul that redemption is in Christ (Rom. 3:24). This raises the question: How does one get into Christ? The answer is found in the writings of Paul. He included himself when he wrote, "Know ye not, that so many of us as were baptized into Jesus Christ were baptized into his death?" (Rom. 6:3). There is only one other place in the Bible that we are told how to get into Christ, and it says the same thing. "For as many of you as have been baptized into Christ have put on Christ" (Gal. 3:27). Before one can be scripturally baptized into Christ he must; believe in Jesus Christ (Mark 16:16); repent of his sins (Acts 2:38); and confess his faith in Christ (Rom. 10:9-10; Acts 8:37). Paul understood this and knew that the power to accomplish this objective was in the gospel. He not only said he was not ashamed of the gospel (Rom. 1:16), but demonstrated his courage in declaring all the counsel of God wherever he went. He proved from the Scriptures again and again that Jesus is the Christ, and the only hope of salvation for sinful man. We are told this is the way he preached in Thessalonica that resulted in some believing and joining with Paul and Silas (Acts 17:2-4). Preaching cannot be effective in saving of souls, the purpose for which God commanded it (1 Cor. 1:21), if it is not based in the Scriptures.

This is an important lesson for all to learn in view of the fact that many do not believe in the hereafter. Many believe that when they die that ends their existence. One thing to remember about the second coming of Christ and the judgment is the surprise it will be to those who believe this false doctrine. There have been scoffers in the past who asked, "Where is the sign of his coming?" (2 Pet. 3:4). They said that all things were continuing as they were from the beginning of creation, which to them proved he was not coming. That was a false assumption, and so is the reasoning of many today who reject the abundance of evidence that Jesus is coming again to judge the world. Let us be as effective as we can be in convincing people of this, and that they will be judged by the words of Jesus who will be the judge. See John 12:48.

In Declaring All the Counsel of God Paul Was Pure From the Blood of All Men

The basis on which Paul could make the statement that he was pure from the blood of all men was the fact he had not shunned to declare all the counsel of God. The implication of this is that any religious teacher who does shrink back from declaring all the counsel of God, through any personal or selfish consideration, in some sense the blood of those he teaches is upon him. When the Jews opposed themselves and blasphemed, Paul told them their blood would be upon their own heads (Acts 18:6).

The same principle was taught in the Old Testament. Consider this statement of the Lord to his people Israel through the prophet Ezekiel, *"Son of man, I have made thee a watchman unto the house of Israel: therefore hear the word at my mouth, and give them warning from me. When I say unto the wicked: Thou shalt surely die; and thou givest him not warning, nor speakest to warn the wicked from his wicked way, to save his life; the same wicked man shall die in his iniquity; but his blood will I require at thine hand. Yet if thou warn the wicked, and he turn not from his wickedness, nor from his wicked way, he shall die in his iniquity; but thou hast delivered thy soul. Again, when a righteous man doth turn from his righteousness, and commit iniquity, and I lay a stumblingblock before him, he shall die: because thou hast not given him warning, he shall die in his sin, and his righteousness which he hath done shall not be remembered; but his blood will I require at thine hand nevertheless if thou warn the righteous man, that the righteous sin not, and he doth not sin he shall surely live, because he is warned; also thou hast delivered thy soul"* (Ezek. 3:17-21). A very similar statement is found in chapter 33:7-9. As watchmen we are to be alert to what is going on for there are many ways God's people are being led astray from the path of righteousness. It is not enough that we see danger when it appears, but we must sound the alarm, warning those who may be affected as well as comforting those who need comfort. Effective preaching necessarily involves warning the wicked to forsake their wicked ways, and the righteous to continue in their righteousness. There is also the need of warning of the ever presence of false teachers who come in sheep's clothing to destroy the flock of God. Only in this way can we be pure from the blood of all men.

Paul's Preaching At Ephesus

Remember that it was to the elders of the church of Ephesus that Paul made the statement that he had not shunned to declare all the counsel of God (Acts 20:27). He taught them there were no gods made with hands, hence their gods were false gods. He wanted them to understand there is only one true and living God, and wrote to them to convince them of that fact (Eph. 4:5). He taught them things concerning the kingdom of God (Acts 19:8). What Paul taught them concerning the kingdom of God was the same thing he taught elsewhere, and also the same as what other inspired men taught, and the same as what Jesus taught.

Jesus used the words "kingdom" and "church" interchangeably when he said to Peter and the rest of the apostles, *"And I say also unto thee, That thou art Peter, and upon this rock I will build my church; and the gates of hell shall not prevail against it. And I will give unto thee the keys of the kingdom of heaven: and what-soever thou shall bind on earth shall be bound in heaven: and whatsoever thou shalt loose on earth shall be loosed in heaven"* (Matt. 16:18-19). The rule of Christ demonstrates the truth that the church and the kingdom are terms used in the Scriptures to refer to those who are subject to his rule. He has a kingdom (John 18:36), and therefore is a king. He is also *"the head over all things to the church which is His body"* (Eph. 1:22-23). When one is obedient to the Lord he is saved from his sins and added by the Lord to his church (Acts 2:38, 47). Paul preached among the Ephesians the kingdom of God. Many believed his message and as a result there was a local church of Christ in that city (Acts 19:8; 20:17). He told the Corinthians he taught the same thing in every church (1 Cor. 14:17). It is evident he did not say the believers in Colossae were *"delivered out of the power of darkness, and translated into the kingdom of God's dear Son"* (Col. 1:13), and then tell the Ephesians they were in the church, but would have to wait until Christ comes again to enter the kingdom.

The Bible teaches that when the end comes Jesus will deliver up the kingdom to the Father (1 Cor. 15:24), and the Bible also tells us that Jesus will present the church to himself a glorious church without spot or blemish (Eph. 5:27). It should be evident from these Bible passages that the kingdom of Christ is now in existence, and every one who is born again of water and of the Spirit enters that kingdom at that time. The notion of many which says that Jesus is coming back to earth some day at which time he will establish his kingdom and rule here on earth for a thousand years is therefore false and should be rejected.

Chapter Seven

Other Reasons Paul Was Effective

He Knew the Value of Using Examples in His Preaching

Example is a powerful way to teach valuable lessons. It is easier to understand a precept if we have an example showing how it applies. Every effective teacher knows the value of example as a teaching method that helps students accomplish their goals or solve problems. God knew that long before man learned it. Therefore we can expect to find his inspired teachers using that method. A careful study of the sermons Paul preached and the letters he wrote will show he successfully used that method. This is demonstrated in two outstanding occasions of his preaching.

In his first letter to the church at Thessalonica he told them, *"For our gospel came not unto you in word only, but also in power, and in the Holy Spirit and in much assurance, as ye know what manner of men we were among you for your sake"* (1 Thess. 1:5). He also reminded them again how he had conducted himself in their presence saying, *"Ye are witnesses, and God also, how holily and justly and unblamably we behaved ourselves among you that believe"* (1 Thess. 2:10). He encouraged the saints at Philippi to follow his example. *"Those things, which ye have both learned, and received, and heard, **and seen in me,** do: and the God of peace will be with you"* (Phil. 4:9). These are a few of the many times he reminded others to follow him. He knew he was not the perfect example for others so in one of his statements on this subject he said, *"Be ye followers of me, even as I also am of Christ"* (1 Cor. 11:1).

Every one who accepts the responsibility of preaching the word should be the kind of person who can encourage others to follow him. Paul wrote to Timothy telling him, *"Let no man despise thy youth; but **be thou an example** of the believers, in word, in conversation, in charity, in spirit, in faith, in purity"* (1 Tim. 4:12). Jesus knew the value of a good example in effectively teaching others, and told his disciples, *"For I have given you an example, that ye should do as I have done to you"* (John 13:15). Consider this statement from the pen of the inspired apostle Peter, *"For even hereunto were ye called: because Christ also suffered for us, leaving us an example, that ye should follow his steps"* (1 Pet. 2:21). Preachers who are effective in winning souls to Christ live the way they are teaching others to live

This Can Help Us Be More Effective in Our Preaching

There are a number of examples of people who were converted to the Lord recorded in the book of Acts. The record of Paul's conversion is found three times—in chapters 9, 22, and 26. Studying these examples and learning what they did to receive salvation and be converted to the Lord is an effective way to teach people of our time what the Lord requires for our salvation. A good way to study these examples is to look at what Jesus told his apostles before he ascended as they carried out the work he gave them to do. Three of the inspired writers tell us of the great commission Jesus gave them. Matthew wrote that he told them to *"go teach all nations, baptizing them in the name of the Father, the Son, and the Holy Spirit, teaching them to observe all things whatsoever I have commanded you"* (Matt. 28:19-20). Mark wrote that he said for them to go preach the gospel to every creature, and said, *"He that believeth and is baptized shall be saved; but he that believeth not shall be damned"* (Mark 16:15-16). Luke's account says that repentance and remission of sins should be preached in his name, beginning at Jerusalem, and that they were to tarry there until they received power from on high (Luke 24:46-49). To learn all the Lord requires of one for salvation we must accept what all of these men wrote on this subject. When we do that we learn that hearing the word of the Lord, believing it, repenting of sins, and being baptized into the name of the Father, the Son, and the Holy Spirit are all requirements, and we have no right to leave out any of them.

The Bible gives us at least nine different examples of some who were converted to him. In every case they heard the gospel preached (specifically mentioned in every case), they believed (expressed or implied), they repented (again expressed or implied), they confessed their faith in Jesus Christ (see Acts 8:37), and they were baptized (baptism is mentioned in every case).

A good and effective way to convince people what is involved in being converted to Christ, and how conversion takes place is to tell of these examples of those who were converted who heard the apostles and other inspired preachers in the long ago. Jesus was talking to the apostles when he promised the Holy Spirit would guide them into all truth (John 16:13). He fulfilled this promise beginning on the first Pentecost following his resurrection and ascension (Acts 2:1-4). The Holy Spirit was guiding them in what they were preaching, and they made no mistakes in what they said. God's Spirit also revealed to the men who wrote the Bible what they were to write, and we have that inspired message to guide us in what we are to preach. Paul wrote to the church of God at Corinth, telling them that the things he wrote to them were the commandments of the Lord (1 Cor. 14:37). In his second letter to Timothy he said, *"all Scripture is given by inspiration of God"* (2 Tim. 3:16-17). Severe consequences await those who add to, take from, pervert or change God's revealed message in any way. This is pointed out in such passages as Revelation 22:18-19; 2 Peter 3:15-16; Galatians 1:8-9; 2 John 9-11.

Paul Knew There Would Be Times it Would Be Necessary to Reprove and Rebuke

He charged Timothy to *"preach the word; be instant in season, out of season; reprove, rebuke, exhort with all longsuffering and doctrine"* (2 Tim. 4:2). The Bible tells us of occasions when Paul did as he here charged Timothy to do. After his conversion to Christ Paul went to many places preaching the gospel. He and Barnabas left Antioch to go on a trip together. One of the first places they went was the island of Cyprus. After preaching in the city of Salamis they went through the island to the city of Paphos. There they found a sorcerer who was a false prophet, a Jew, whose name was Bar-jesus. He was with a man who was interested in what Paul had to say, and tried to turn him away from the faith.

Paul reproved and rebuked him, and by the power of the Holy Spirit given to him struck him blind for a season. Paul also rebuked Peter when he came to Antioch because he would not eat with the Gentiles, but withdrew and separated himself when some disciples came from Jerusalem. The reason he gave for this action was that Peter was to be blamed and had not walked uprightly according to the truth of the gospel. It should be pointed out that it was not because of some personality conflict between Paul and Peter nor some vendetta that he rebuked Peter, but the truth of the gospel was involved. What all Christians of today need to learn from this is when we reprove or rebuke someone we need to be sure it is because the truth of the gospel is involved, and that they are in danger of losing their own souls and/or influencing others to do wrong.

When the need arose Paul did not hesitate to dispute with those who were in the wrong. On one occasion there were those who taught that Gentiles must be circumcised after the manner of Moses in order to be saved. He disputed with them about the matter (Acts 15:1-2). Later Peter withdrew himself from eating with Gentiles when certain brethren from Jerusalem came to Antioch and Paul withstood him to the face because he walked not uprightly according to the truth of the gospel (Gal. 2:11-14).

He Knew How to Deal With Persecution and Criticism

Prior to his conversion Paul had been heavily involved in persecuting Christ and everything that had to do with him. He was present and giving his consent to the stoning of Stephen (Acts 7). He was on his way to Damascus with letters from the high priest to bind any who were of the Way and bring them to Jerusalem to be punished when the Lord appeared to him (Acts 9). After his conversion to the Lord he became the persecuted. He was beaten with many stripes, put in prison, shipwrecked, and endured many hardships for the Lord. He mentions a number of these things in his second letter to the church at Corinth (2 Cor. 11:23-28). He followed the example of the Lord in this and gloried in tribulations (Rom. 5:3), knowing that tribulation works patience. One reason he endured such treatment was that the elect may obtain the salvation that is in Christ (2 Tim. 2:10). Effective gospel preachers of any age will endure such treatment that they may help those they teach to obtain the salvation that is in Christ.

Paul Genuinely Cared for All Men, Especially Those Whom He Taught the Gospel

Immediately after Paul was converted to Christ he began preaching that which he had so vigorously opposed before. Feeling a strong compulsion to preach he later wrote, *"yea, woe is unto me, if I preach not the gospel"* (1 Cor. 9:16). Following that statement he told of his willingness to become all things to all men that by all means he might save some. He urged these same people that, whatever they did to do it to the glory of God, even as he sought to please all men in all things, not seeking his own profit, but that of many, that many may be saved (1 Cor. 10:31-33).

Perhaps no other human being ever suffered more for the Lord than this great apostle. He made mention of some of the things he suffered in his writings, and said that whether he suffered or was comforted it was for their consolation and salvation (2 Cor. 1:6). He listed a number of things he endured for the gospel's sake, including the care of all the churches (2 Cor. 11:23-28). While the primary concern was for the salvation of their souls, he also had a deep concern for their physical well being. The church at Philippi sent gifts to Paul by Epaphroditus while he was in prison. While he was there he became sick and almost died. After he recovered sufficiently Paul sent him back that they might see him again and rejoice. What Paul desired in all of this was fruit that may abound to their account (Phil. 2:25-30; 4:17-18). There are numerous other statements by and about Paul that shows it was not the possessions of the people he wanted, but the people themselves for the Lord. He told the Corinthians, *"for I seek not yours, but you"* (2 Cor. 12:14). The Thessalonian Christians were dear to him; they were his glory and joy (1 Thess. 2:8, 20). This was true of his feelings toward all other disciples of the Lord, especially those he knew, and had taught the gospel. Those in every generation who would be effective in teaching the most important message ever taught would do well to follow this example of the apostle Paul.

Effective Preaching and Prayer

Before Saul was converted to Christ he was a man of prayer. While he was on his way to Damascus with letters from the high priest to bind any he found who were of the Way, whether men or women, he would bring them bound to Jerusalem, he met the

Lord and talked with him. The Lord told him to go to the city and he would be told what he must do. Subsequently the Lord appeared to a disciple named Ananias, instructing him to seek for Saul. During the three-day period that elapsed, Saul was without sight, and neither ate nor drank, and the Lord told Ananias that he prayed. (Acts 9:1-11). Prayer continued to be a major part of his life after he became a disciple of the Lord.

He prayed for his Jewish brethren. His prayer for them was that they might be saved. *"Brethren, my heart's desire and prayer to God for Israel is that they might be saved. For I bear them record that they have a zeal of God, but not according to knowledge. For they being ignorant of God's righteousness, and going about to establish their own righteousness, have not submitted themselves unto the righteousness of God"* (Rom. 10:1-3). He not only prayed for their salvation, but also was willing to do whatever was necessary within the bounds of the word of God to bring this about. He said that unto the Jews he was willing to become as a Jew, that he might gain the Jews. (1 Cor. 9:20).

He prayed for his brethren in the Lord. On behalf of the Ephesian Christians he prayed that they might be strengthened in the inner man. *"For this cause I bow my knees unto the Father of our Lord Jesus Christ, of whom the whole family in heaven and earth is named, that he would grant you, according to the riches of his glory, to be strengthened with might by his Spirit in the inner man"* (Eph. 3:14-16). Later in this same letter he urged them to *"be strong in the Lord, and in the power of his might"* (Eph. 6:10). It is the inner man that needs strength to win the battles against Satan and the powers of evil. He was interested in their physical well being, but it is evident he was more concerned about their souls for they are of more value in the sight of God. He prayed for the Philippians that their love would abound (Phil. 1:9), and for the Colossians that they may be filled with the knowledge of God's will in all wisdom and spiritual understanding (Col. 1:9). It should be evident from these statements that Paul was deeply concerned about their souls, and prayed that they might live so they would be saved.

He prayed for those who forsook him when he was on trial. His prayer for them was that the fact they did not stand by him would not be laid to their charge (2 Tim. 4:16). Stephen prayed in a similar way when he was stoned to death, an event Paul witnessed (Acts 7:60). Both of these men were following the example and instructions of Jesus Christ. He told his disciples to love their enemies and pray for those who despitefully used them and persecuted them (Matt. 5:44). While Jesus was on the cross, he prayed for those who crucified him, saying, *"Father, forgive them; for they know not what they do"* (Luke 23:34).

He asked the Colossians to pray for him that God would open to them a door of utterance that he may speak the mystery of Christ. From other passages we learn that the mystery of Christ included the fact that Gentiles were offered salvation the same as the Jews, and on the same conditions (see Eph. 3:3-6). Doors of opportunity to preach Christ were opened to him, and he took advantage of every one of them. He delayed his coming to Corinth because a door was opened to him in Ephesus. Here is what he said about that, *"But I will tarry at Ephesus until Pentecost. For a great door and effectual is opened unto me, and there are many adversaries"* (1 Cor. 16:9). The report he and Barnabas gave to the church at Antioch when they returned from their first tour of preaching the gospel included this fact. *"And when they were come, and had gathered the church together, they rehearsed all that God had done with them, and how he had opened the door of faith unto the Gentiles"* (Acts 14:27). Effective preachers of the gospel today will pray for doors to be opened. Let us make sure that, when we pray for God to open doors, we will be ready to preach when he answers our prayer.

In his final words of exhortation and encouragement to the Corinthians he wrote, *"Now I pray to God that ye do no evil"* (2 Cor. 13:7). He did not pray this prayer that he might appear approved by them, but that they should do that which was honest. What concern for those he loved in the Lord!

Paul knew he needed the prayers of his brethren. He did not ask them to pray that he may be delivered from physical suffering, but that he may speak boldly the mystery of Christ. Knowing that he would be called upon to give a defense of his teaching concerning Christ, even before a king, he asked the Ephesian Christians to pray for him *"that I may open my mouth boldly, to make known the mystery of the gospel, For which I am an ambassador in bonds: that therein I may speak boldly, as I ought to speak"* (Eph. 6:19-20). On several occasions as he traveled from place to place preaching it is said that he spoke boldly. Soon after his conversion he tried to join himself to the disciples at Jerusalem, but they were not sure his conversion was genuine until Barnabas told the brethren he had preached boldly at Damascus in the name of Jesus (Acts 9:27). Immediately after this we are told that at Jerusalem he continued to speak boldly in the name of Jesus, disputing against the Grecians, and they went about to kill him; but that did not deter him from continuing to preach boldly in the name of Jesus. He spoke boldly at Antioch in Pisidia, at Iconium, and while a prisoner at Rome (Acts 13:46; 14:3; 28:31). It was because of the hope he had in Christ Jesus that he spoke boldly to the end Christ may be magnified in his body whether by life or by death (Phil. 1:20; 2 Cor. 3:12; 1 Thess. 2:2). To speak boldly is to speak freely, openly, and plainly with confidence and without fear. The boldness with which Paul spoke, even when he was in prison, gave confidence to others to be bold in their speaking the word without fear (Phil. 1:12-14).

Even before Paul began preaching the unsearchable riches of Christ other disciples were praying that they may speak the word with all boldness (Acts 4:29). They were speaking to a hostile crowd at this time, and the Bible says that when they prayed the place where they were was shaken, and they spoke the word of God with all boldness (Acts 4:30-31). It should be pointed out that some of those who heard the apostles preach on this occasion threatened them with imprisonment if they continued preaching that salvation was in the name of Jesus whom they said was raised from the dead. The reply of Peter and John was this: *"We cannot but speak the things which we have seen and heard"* (Acts 4:20). Later all the apostles were threatened in the same way, and this is their reaction, *"Then Peter and the other apostles answered and said, We ought to obey God rather than men"* (Acts 5:29). Those who heard them make these statements wanted to kill them but were persuaded not to do so at that time. They did beat them and charged them not to preach or teach any more in the name of Jesus, but they departed from the council and rejoiced that they were counted worthy to suffer for Jesus' name (5:33-41).

There is a great need for this kind of preaching today when so many are more interested in hearing what makes them feel good than in what they need in order to be right with God. Paul warned Timothy of the need of speaking the truth boldly for the time would come when they would not endure sound doctrine, *"but after their own lusts shall they heap to themselves teachers, having itching ears; And they shall turn away their ears from the truth, and shall be turned unto fables"* (2 Tim. 4:3-4). The existence of the many false religions give testimony to the fact that Paul was right in describing conditions that would happen after he departed this life. We can know by reading what Paul wrote by the inspiration of the Holy Spirit what is involved in preaching the truth boldly, and the necessity of such preaching in order to be effective in saving the lost. Is there a sincere preacher among us who thinks he does not need the prayers of faithful brethren that he may speak boldly as he ought to speak? While preachers need "a happy recollection of the things they have prepared to say" we should also pray they will speak it boldly as they ought.

Boldness in preaching is not the same as arrogance. To be arrogant is to have a feeling of self-importance. It is a similar idea of pride, or exalting oneself above others, and is the opposite of humility. God has always required us to be humble, and has praised those who were humble. An Old Testament prophet wrote, *"He hath shewed thee, O man, what is good; and what doth the LORD require of thee, but to do justly, and to love mercy, and to walk **humbly** with thy God?"* (Mic. 6:8). Jesus taught that we must humble ourselves and become as little children in order to enter the kingdom of heaven (Matt. 18:3-4). Paul taught the brethren at Corinth that they needed to learn not to think above that which is written, that they should not be puffed up one against another. He then asked some pointed questions to help them realize they had nothing except what they received, and since they received it why did they glory as if they did not receive it (1 Cor. 4:6-7)? Paul had a thorn in the flesh he called a messenger of Satan, to buffet him, lest he should be exalted above measure (2 Cor. 12:7). No doubt there are many in the world today who present themselves as preachers who need a thorn or two. The effective preacher of Paul's day recognized that whatever he had, talents, ability, material possessions, etc., he received it from the Lord, and did not have any basis on which to glory in himself.

Paul, like David, knew that his help came from the Lord. He told Agrippa that some had gone about to kill him. He then said he obtained help from God, and continued witnessing to that day (Acts 26:21-22). He had confidence the Lord would deliver him from every evil work, and preserve him unto the heavenly kingdom (2 Tim. 4:18). Few preachers have suffered for the cause of Christ as Paul did, but all who experience any persecutions or tribulations should take courage by such an example, and put their confidence in the Lord knowing he will reward all such with eternal life. When we consider the influence Satan continues to have over the people of this time how can any of us hope to be effective in winning souls to Christ without the help of the Lord?

Paul was an effective preacher because he knew that men were sinners, and that God's remedy for sin was the gospel. He also knew that to be effective he must teach sinners what God requires in our obedience and how Christians must live to receive the eternal reward he has promised. Therefore he presented the information they needed, and then admonished them to render the obedience. An example of this is found in the case of the people of Athens. Paul entered their city and found a number of gods they were worshiping, including one to the unknown god. Paul then declared unto them the God they did not know. He gave evidence of the existence of the God who made the world and all things in it. He concluded by saying that God now commands all men everywhere to repent thus calling upon them to believe in and obey him. Some of them did believe, but some did not. All the apostles used this same method the first time the gospel was preached. They preached to the people in Jerusalem on Pentecost that they had crucified Jesus, but that God had raised him up and made him both Lord and Christ. They were pricked in their hearts, and asked what they must do. They were told to repent, and be baptized in the name of Jesus Christ for the remission of their sins, and were exhorted to save themselves from that crooked generation (Acts 2:22-40). The inspired preachers of the first century taught people what they should do in order to be what God would have them be, and then exhorted them to do it. This is essential in being made free from sin. Paul wrote to the Christians at Rome, *"But God be thanked, that ye were the servants of sin, but ye have obeyed from the heart that form of doctrine which was delivered you, being then made free from sin, ye became the servants of righteousness"* (Rom. 6:17-18). It should be evident from this passage in the Bible that one must know what he is obeying and do it from the heart in order to have forgiveness of sins. One of the reasons some do not remain faithful to the Lord is they have not been sufficiently taught before they are exhorted to obey the gospel. There is a limit to what preachers can do in such situations, but we should do all we can to make sure we instruct sinners what the Lord requires and then exhort them to obey from the heart. Christians also need to be taught and exhorted to continue to cleave to the Lord. Barnabas did this when he went to Antioch (Acts 11:23).

Conclusion

It is my humble prayer that all who read this book, whether a preacher of the gospel or not, will learn something that will enable them to recognize what it takes for preaching to be effective and accept only that which is according to the word of God. May this material help us look to the word of God as our complete and final source of authority in all we accept, practice, and teach in all our religious activities. May our lives be governed completely by what is found in the Scriptures that are given by the inspiration of God, and at the end of our lives be able to say, as Paul did, *"For I am now ready to be offered, and the time of my departure is at hand. I have fought a good fight, I have finished my course, I have kept the faith: Henceforth there is laid up for me a crown of righteousness, which the Lord, the righteous judge, shall give me at that day: and not to me only, but unto all them also that love his appearing"* (2 Tim. 4:6-8).

www.ingramcontent.com/pod-product-compliance
Lightning Source LLC
Chambersburg PA
CBHW031525040426
42445CB00009B/403